COLOR A
MAGICK SPELL

26 PICTURE SPELLS TO COLOR & MANIFEST

HELGA HEDGEWALKER
WITH ESTELLE DANIELS

FIRST EDITION
First Printing, 2018

Art by Helga Hedgewalker
Book design by Rebecca Zins
Cover design by Kevin R. Brown

Llewellyn Publications is a registered
trademark of Llewellyn Worldwide Ltd.

ISBN 978-0-7387-5357-7

Llewellyn Publications
A Division of Llewellyn Worldwide Ltd.
2143 Wooddale Drive
Woodbury, MN 55125-2989
www.llewellyn.com

Printed in the United States of America

*This book is dedicated to the Muse, without
whose blessing and inspiration no art would
be possible. Deep and sincerest thanks.*

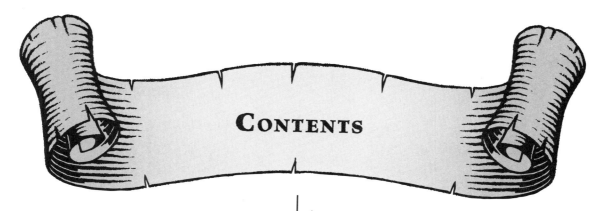

CONTENTS

Appendices

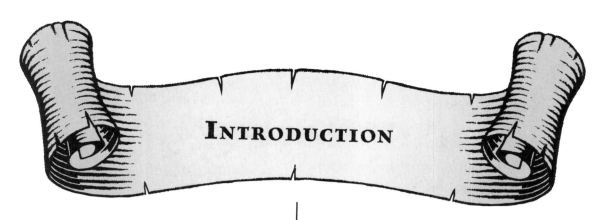

INTRODUCTION

THIS BOOK IS like a cake mix for spellwork. We have assembled and pre-mixed the main ingredients; add a few fresh ingredients of your own, mix and "bake," and in the end you have a completed spell.

Many people do not have the time to study spellwork and assemble all the various ingredients for the standard spells a person might need in everyday life. In this book are twenty-six picture spells. These spells cover much of what a person might encounter in life. They contain symbols and images that evoke the energies of the spell; when activated, they can be a powerful force for positive change in a person's life. The images are based on the twenty-two Major Arcana, or trumps of the tarot. We chose specific aspects of each card, so they may be different than a more standard tarot deck. We also made images for the four aces of each suit of the Minor Arcana, to reference the elements and qualities they represent.

These spells are not to be used lightly. They are for times when you need extra effort to accomplish an important goal. Coloring each picture will take time. You have to judge whether the time and effort spent is worth what you want to accomplish.

Just what is a spell, anyway? A spell is like a concentrated wish or prayer. If you have something you want or need, then decide if putting time and energy into it is worth your while. Assemble what you need, go to a quiet place where you will not be interrupted, and clear your mind. Place a circle of protection around yourself and then work your spell. This circle of protection is not because these spells are dangerous; it is because you are concentrating, and you want to protect yourself from outside influences as you work. You will

want to keep out any other energies that might clash or be at cross purposes with your intent. The circle of protection is like a psychic cleanup of your environment, allowing you to start with a clean workspace for your spell.

This is more than a collection of pretty pictures. These images are designed for use in ritual spellwork as well as artistic contexts. Each image was carefully designed to contain many images and symbols that evoke certain themes. These are not the only images that may apply to the topic addressed; they are just the ones we have chosen. We have drawn primarily on the images and symbols of astrology, runes, Western culture, and classical, Celtic, and Norse mythology. They are assemblies of images, each designed to reinforce and integrate with each other. Purists will say you shouldn't mix systems—that runes and astrology don't belong together, for example. But each is a powerful symbolic system, and each deals with similar themes. We have chosen to combine the symbols here to create what we feel will work for most anyone. Don't expect to resonate with every element in every picture. Pick out those images and symbols that speak most strongly to you and focus on those. For instance, you might decide to color those elements the brightest, put some sequins or rhinestones around them, or give them a glitter treatment. Alternatively, you might glue some other images over any parts you don't like. After all, this is all about your magickal intent.

Spells are accomplished with the help of your subconscious. Unfortunately, most people are not directly in contact with their subconscious. Over the years, certain techniques have been found to be effective for

contacting the subconscious and allowing a person to "work magick." One method is to use ritual. We have included a simple but powerful circle casting that not only will provide protection for you as you work, but will also allow you to access your subconscious and therefore effectively accomplish your intent. If you have your own circle or ritual you prefer to use, feel free to use that.

You send your energies into the picture through the act of coloring. By coloring your energies into the picture, you energize the images. Moreover, the energized images are sent out to the universe by your subconscious as you color. Your act of coloring energizes the potentials in the symbols, and while you color your subconscious integrates the elements into a coherent spell. As you color and look at the symbols and colors and think about what you want and what you are doing, your subconscious is getting the message on many levels—physically through your hand doing the coloring, mentally by seeing the images and colors, emotionally by thinking about what you want and why you want it, spiritually through the power of the images and symbols you are seeing and coloring—and your actions are providing the energy needed to send your wishes to the universe and accomplish your purpose. It's a magickal process.

It should be emphasized that this form of spellcasting is designed to be fun. You are allowing your inner child to play while you ask the universe for something that is important for you. We all colored when we were young, and this energy can add to the effectiveness of spellwork if properly accessed. The subconscious likes to play, so let it play as you color and think about what you mean to accomplish. Then it can go about the business of making magick for you in a spirit of sacred fun.

Creating Your Spell—
The Condensed Version

1. Know what you want and why. Save the "how" for the universe.

2. Gather your supplies and prepare a clean, sacred, quiet space where you won't be disturbed.

3. Take a ritual bath (or perform some other self-purification), then ground and center.

4. Cast a circle or otherwise acknowledge that you are in sacred space (see our circle on page 8 or use your own).

5. Follow the ritual for the image you choose, coloring and doing anything else you need.

6. Complete the project and take down the circle (see page 10).

7. Log your progress in the spellworking log on page 139.

8. Keep your project where you can see it until the spell has manifested.

9. Once the spell has manifested, destroy or otherwise decommission the spell.

In the appendices we have included fuller explanations for colors, runes, and astrological symbols. This can help in understanding our meanings or suggesting additional symbols to further customize your spell. There is also a spellworking log to record your spells as you do them. This is not required, but it can help you realize what you have accomplished with your spellwork.

Creating Your Spell—
The Fuller Explanation

First, you need to know what you want. Know what you are asking the universe to help you with and why. As the old saying goes, "Be careful what you ask for; you might get it!" If you can state clearly and concisely what you want, you will get better results. However, you should be careful not to be too specific or you will limit your results.

As an example, if you need a car, asking for a safe, reliable vehicle is acceptable. Asking for a red convertible sports car probably will not get you what you need. Be careful to phrase your wish in positive terms such as "I will be safe and secure in my life and home environment." Avoid statements with "no" or "not," such as "I don't want anyone to hurt or harm me." The subconscious doesn't always hear "no" in its many forms, and a spell using "no" or "not" can backfire.

Form a clear statement of intent. This can be as elaborate or as simple as you like. The possibilities are endless. Be positive in your request.

An example:

Father/Mother God, I ask, in your name, to grant me _____. May it come to me in the fullness of time. Thank you for your blessings.

As you work, visualize your spell coming true. Visualize the results of your spell, not the exact mechanism.

Plan your spell. Decide on when you will do it. You can use astrology to help find the most potent time or just do it when convenient. Make an appointment with yourself and keep it. Gather together whatever items you will need: things needed for the circle and art supplies needed to color the picture. Then also make a list of things you need to do to help accomplish this spell. It does no good to do the best job spell in the world unless you also get the job listings on the internet, make a few calls, send out résumés, and get dressed and go to the interviews. Jobs do not drop out of the sky; nor does money, love, etc. You have to get yourself to the right place to get what you need and be open to finding what you asked for in unusual places. If you do a love spell and an attractive person strikes up a conversation in the grocery line, go with the flow. Don't limit yourself.

Be careful not to harm anyone with your spell. Harm comes in many forms. These spells cannot be used for purposes of revenge or power over someone else, which includes a love spell for a specific person. If you want love, be open to whoever comes. You don't have to say yes to whoever comes along, but you should not say "I want so-and-so to fall madly in love with me." That is coercive magick, and it can backfire badly. If you feel you have been hurt or wronged, you certainly have the right to call the universe's attention to it and request justice. But let the universe decide what form it will take and when or if it will happen.

If you are doing a spell on behalf of someone else, make sure you have their specific permission to do so. Remember, whatever you put out returns to you threefold, so think about what you are putting out.

Before you do the spell at the time and place you have set aside for it, first do some sort of self-purification. This can be as elaborate as a ritual bath or as simple as smudging ("bathing" in smoke from incense or smoldering herbs like sage or sweetgrass) or visualizing yourself within a white or golden halo. Light some appropriate incense and put on some tranquil music, if you like. Cast a circle for protection (explained on page 9). Invite your guardian angel/god/gods/goddesses/spirit helpers to join you. Speak your affirmation clearly, loudly, proudly. Singing or chanting also works. Color your spell page while concentrating on the symbols and colors you are using. Formulate a personal affirmation to write at the bottom of the spell, if that appeals to you. Feel free to embellish your art with pasted-in photos, beads, glitter, fabric, small plastic toys, or whatever seems appropriate. Have fun with your spell project! Let your inner child come out and play. When finished, thank your invited spirit guests for coming and close your circle.

Hang your magickal art somewhere special where you will see it and be able to meditate on it for a few minutes each day. Repeat your affirmation out loud. Visualize your wish coming true. Do not take it down until either your goal is achieved or you realize that the goal is no longer important to you. It can take anywhere from a few minutes to a few months to achieve your goal. It depends upon what you want and how the universe chooses to accomplish it.

When you have gotten what you wanted or outgrown that need or wish, your spell art is finished. Thank the universe and deity/deities, then ritually bury, burn, or cast away the remnants of your spell. This can mean you actually bury or burn the artwork itself, or you can just symbolically burn away the energies of your spell contained within the artwork by cleansing it with sage or incense. If you just get rid of the spell energies, you can keep the artwork as a pretty picture.

You can have more than one spell in the works at one time, but be careful not to burn yourself out. You should do only one spell per session. Start a new circle and process for each separate spell. You do not have to complete the spell in only one session; just be sure you cast a circle each session. The point is not to take forever to color the drawing. You are adding your energies and intent to the drawing by coloring and adding other things. If you need three or more spells at a time, it might be best to sort your priorities and concentrate on the one or two most pressing needs first. When those are accomplished, then move on to other things.

The Magickal Circle

The following instructions are for a circle we have created for these images. If you have another way of ritually grounding, centering, and finding your sacred space that you prefer, use that.

Tools Needed

- a wand (as simple as a branch from a tree or an elaborately created item or something in between)—it should be longer than your hand but shorter than your arm, and it should be something you feel comfortable directing your energy through

- a bowl of water

- a bowl of salt

- incense and a holder (stick incense is easiest to use)

- a lighter or matches

- a candle to light at the start of the circle, either a neutral color or one that reinforces the spell; always place your candle in a holder to catch any dripping wax

- an image of a deity, angel, or saint (optional)

- whatever art supplies you need to color and decorate your image

You need to have a clear, quiet space to work in. Be sure there is enough room for your project as well as the ritual items. They do not have to be on the same surface. You can make the circle include however much space you need. Close the curtains, turn off the phone, and lock the door to minimize interruptions.

Find east, or where the sun comes up. Turn clockwise a quarter turn for each of the other directions—south, west, and north—and then back to east.

Gather all your materials in the place where you will work. Ritually cleanse and prepare yourself. Take a deep, cleansing breath, and begin.

Casting the Circle

Move to the east and use your wand to draw an imaginary line clockwise around your ritual area. You can make a circle in one room and in your mind expand it to include other rooms or your entire house. Once you return to the east, pause and feel the energy of the circle you have drawn. Then lay down your wand and pick up the water bowl.

Hold a hand over the water and feel your energy flowing into it. Say:

I cleanse this water of any impurities or negative influences so that it may wash clean.

Put the water bowl down.

Take the bowl of salt. Hold a hand over the salt and feel your energy flowing into it. Say:

I cleanse this salt of any impurities or negative influences so that it may properly ground energies.

Then take a pinch of salt and drop it into the water, swirl it gently around, and say:

May this salt and water combine to cleanse and purify this sacred space.

Take the mixture and move to the east. Sprinkle a few drops in the east and move around the circle clockwise, pausing at each quarter to sprinkle a few more drops. As you do this, at each quarter say:

I cleanse this circle so that it may be pure and ready for my magickal purpose.

Return the water bowl and take the incense. Light the incense and say:

I invite the power of fire to energize me for my ritual.

After the incense has burned for a bit, blow out the flame and see the smoke curling up. Say:

I charge the power of air to guide me in my magickal rite.

Take the lit incense around the circle clockwise, saying at each quarter:

Fire and air, I charge you to consecrate this circle for my magickal purpose.

Return the incense to its holder. Allow it to burn while you color your image. If it burns out, you can start another stick or just let it go.

Take your wand and move to the east. Hold your wand up and say this blessing at each quarter, putting the appropriate name at each quarter:

Guardians of the East (South, West, North), I ask for your aid and protection in this magickal rite. Hail and welcome!

Move to each quarter in turn and repeat the blessing. Then move back to the east and say:

This circle is cast to aid me in my magickal working. May the blessing and protection of the universe aid and guide me.

At this point, you may call on your deity, guardian angel, or spirit guides to be with you as you work your magick. This is optional. Use whatever words you like. As an example, you might say:

I call on my guardian angel to be present with me in this circle and to guide and aid me as I work this magick.

Now your circle is complete.

This is the place in the ritual where you work your magick by decorating your image. You are protected while you color and decorate your image and work your magick. You can finish the image in one sitting or do it over several sittings. But when you are finished with this session, whether you finish the entire image or not, you must then take down the circle. If you start another session, you must remake the circle before you restart work on your image. This is to keep your magickal energies contained and free of outside influences.

9

Taking Down the Circle

Thank your deity, guardian angel, or spirit guide for attending and send them on their way. Use whatever words you feel comfortable with. As an example, you might say:

I thank my guardian angel for being here with me in this circle. Thank you for your aid and guidance, and I ask for your blessing as you depart to your blessed realms.

Take your wand and move to the east. Hold your wand up and say at each quarter in turn:

Guardians of the East (South, West, North), I thank you for your guidance and protection in this circle. May there be peace between us always, and as you depart I bid you hail and farewell.

Return to the east and again visualize the circle you drew. Take the wand and cut through the circle, severing it and drawing the energies back into yourself as you say:

The circle is open but unbroken. May love and light guide and protect me all my days.

Display your spell art somewhere appropriate.

Symbology and Meaning of the Spell Images

Each image states the main idea at the top. At the bottom of each is a blank area for you to use as you wish. There you can write your intentions, the names of those you wish to help, symbols or affirmations that have special meaning for you, or anything else you can think of. It is up to you to color and add whatever you need to personalize these drawings.

There is no right or wrong way to color the images. Use whatever media are available. What matters is that you are coloring your energies and intent into the picture. This unlocks the power of the symbols to send your spell forth into the universe. You can color the whole image or only the parts that seem important to you. You do not have to finish the coloring in one session, though that is certainly possible. The point is to color the design as it seems appropriate to you for this purpose. It becomes a case of getting what you need, not what you want—just like the Rolling Stones said.

Each spell begins with a brief explanation that outlines the picture's symbols and their meanings.

There are so many gods and goddesses that can be associated with each picture, through many systems of correspondences, that it would take up too much space to include them all—and then inevitably someone would discover one we left out. We chose one particular deity for each picture, but you can substitute whoever you like.

These spells will work if you are clear in your intent and follow the steps outlined above.

0 • NEW BEGINNINGS

NEW BEGINNINGS: the time when things are just hatched and all possibilities are available for you to choose among them.

The situation is formless and new, ready for you to shape it into what you want or need. You have the ability to rise above the past and make something new of yourself, your life, your situation.

This ritual is best done while the moon is waxing between new and full.

The Symbols

We chose symbols that have been used for new beginnings throughout various cultures. If you have others, feel free to draw or paste them in for yourself.

A pair of hands holding soil from which grows a new seedling shows that things are just starting out, ready to be shaped by the forces of nature and you.

The sun is the source of all light and energy in our solar system, and it is the sun that shines and causes the plants to grow.

Shells of a cracked egg. Something has hatched; what could it be, and what will grow from it?

Butterflies are the end result of metamorphosis and new life that goes out into the world to make a new generation.

Look for the glyph for the astrological sign Aries—the first sign of the zodiac, the beginning of the astrological wheel.

Find the rune Berkano, symbolizing beginnings and birth.

See the new moon, symbolizing a fresh start.

Look for the sprouted seed, the beginning of growing life.

Ritual for New Beginnings

Suggested Colors

Green is a color of new growth.

Gold, yellow, and orange are the colors of the sun, the source of all energy in our solar system. They symbolize the endless power the sun has, and that power can be converted to energy, growth, and possibility.

Brown symbolizes the fertility of the earth and the bounty it can bring.

Blue is the color of the sky and calm decision-making and deliberation as you contemplate the possibilities of your new beginning.

Special Supplies
- a white candle
- a gold or yellow candle
- candle holders

To Work This Spell

Light the two candles and invite Kwan Yin to help birth your new beginning.

Here is an invocation that can bring Kwan Yin to help you:

> *Kwan Yin, mother of mercy and compassion,*
> *grant me a new beginning, a way to*
> *start over, to put aside the past.*
> *Help me make good and healthy choices—*
> *choices for myself*
> *choices for my life*
> *choices for my situation—*
> *that I may begin anew and*
> *make a better life for myself.*

Color and decorate the New Beginnings page.

Write your personal affirmation in the box at the bottom of the page.

Say the affirmation out loud seven times (or chant it, sing it, or shout it multiple times) to empower the spell.

When finished, thank Kwan Yin and whatever other deities or elements you have called upon for attending on your behalf.

> *Merciful Kwan Yin,*
> *I thank you for your help*
> *in birthing my new beginning.*
> *Watch over and guide me in my new endeavors*
> *and help me to keep making good choices—*
> *good choices for myself,*
> *good choices in my life,*
> *good choices for my situation.*

Close your circle and relax, confident that you can make a new beginning for yourself. This time things will turn out well.

NEW BEGINNINGS

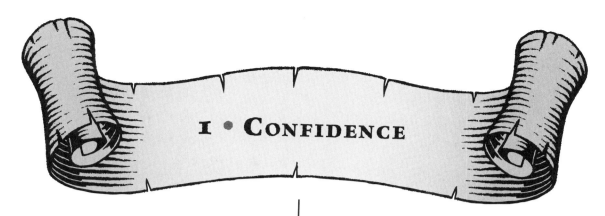

1 • CONFIDENCE

CONFIDENCE: the strength to get up each morning and face the day having the self-respect that makes life a joy to live. It is the knowledge that you are a loved and valuable member of society.

The confidence in your ability to make good choices and bring about changes necessary to meet your goals is the very foundation of magick and spellwork. Gaining confidence in yourself and your connection to the Divine is a starting point. You have to believe in your inherent goodness as a person, and you have to believe and know that magick can and does happen. When you do, amazingly wonderful things in life can and do occur!

Brigid (Bride, Brigantia, Bridget, Brigandu): the triple goddess whose name means "bright arrow" or "bright one." Beloved throughout Celtic lands as the patron of smithcraft and battle, poetry and inspiration, healing and medicine, Brigid is a solar goddess, and fire is one of her most important symbols/elements.

The Symbols

We chose symbols that have been used for confidence throughout various cultures. If you have others, feel free to draw or paste them in for yourself.

Five-pointed star: As Aleister Crowley says, "Every man and every woman is a star." You play the leading role in the drama of your life. You are the star! The five-pointed star we use is a modified pentacle representing the known cosmos and elements of earth, air, fire, water, and spirit (at the top, connecting with heaven) centered and

in balance in the universe. It can also represent the five senses, or humankind, or a man or woman with arms and legs outstretched (a position of power and balance). The pentacle is thought to bestow protection and balance to the person who invokes or wears one. Within the pentacle ring are a series of five affirmations:

> My _____ is beautiful!
> I like myself because _____.
> I am very talented at _____.
> I am respected in _____.
> I am really good at _____.

These are very powerful statements to help you take a fresh look at what a special and unique person you are and how important your place is in this life.

A blazing sun symbolizes your life force and vibrant energy that shines for everyone to see everywhere you go. It is your aura, your spiritual connection to all the living things around you.

Stars, moons, suns, and comets show we are each made from ancient star stuff. No one who has ever lived or ever will live is more or less important than you are right this moment.

Look for the astrological symbols for the sun and Leo, a sign of confidence, creativity, and leadership.

Find the rune Sowilo, which means victory, confidence, health, and vitality.

Ritual for Confidence

Suggested Colors

Yellow is a good color for confidence, vibrant energy, and a sunny disposition.

Gold is a color of leadership, royalty, and wealth.

Orange is a color of creativity. Be a creator!

Red is the color of courage and action.

White is a color of honesty, balance, and purity.

Special Supplies

- a large mirror
- a flattering photo or other small portrait of yourself or an image of the goal that you need confidence in attaining
- 3 red candles

To Work This Spell

Light the first red candle and invite Brigid, the triple goddess, to give you strength, inspiration, and healing. A favorite Brigid invocation is:

> *Brigid before me,*
> *Brigid to my right hand,*
> *Brigid behind me,*
> *Brigid to my left hand,*
> *Brigid above me,*
> *Brigid below me,*
> *Brigid within me,*
> *Brigid be with me!*
> —by Steven Posch
> (used with permission)

Color and decorate the Confidence page. Draw or paste in an image of yourself or your goal at the center of the star. Make sure it is an image that makes you feel attractive, healthy, smart, and vibrant. Allow yourself to be proud of this person (or goal) you have chosen to manifest. (As an optional suggestion, color the flames of the sun to match the colors you would like your aura to have. Ideally, these colors should be clear and bright.)

Take some time to come up with the best answer to each statement: My _____ is beautiful! I like myself because _____, etc. Fill in the blanks around the pentacle.

Light the second red candle and repeat the Brigid invocation.

Write your personal affirmation in the box at the bottom of the page. Say the affirmation out loud nine times (or chant it, sing it, or shout it multiple times) to empower the spell.

Light the third red candle and repeat the Brigid invocation.

Spend some time looking at yourself in the mirror by the light of the three candles. Look long and hard until you see there the person you have always wanted to be. You are that person! The triple goddess is there with you whenever you need her; she is a part of you, and you are a part of her. Know that you are a spark of the infinite light. You shine like the sun.

When finished, thank Brigid and whatever other deities or elements you have called upon for attending on your behalf.

Close your circle and relax, confident that you are an extremely worthwhile and lovable person.

Display your art where you can see it and appreciate it. Smile every time you look at it!

Know that it is a portrait of the true you and that good things are coming your way.

CONFIDENCE ♌

I like myself because... is beautiful! ... My ... I am really good at ... I am respected in ... I am very talented at ...

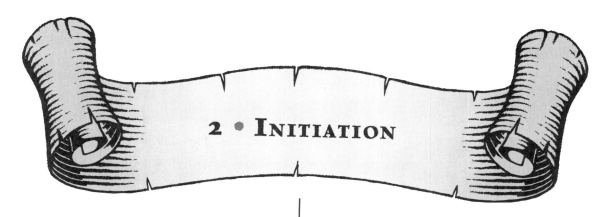

2 • INITIATION

INITIATION: a ceremony performed to let a candidate experience first-hand secret, sacred mysteries.

Initiation often involves some sort of death-and-rebirth symbolism that triggers a change that can only be learned through doing, not talking or reading. Everyone who has gone through the rite then has a common bonding experience, and the initiate thereby becomes part of the inner group.

Initiation is not something to seek lightly. It is a powerful experience that needs to come when the candidate is ready. If done correctly, it will re-wire the way your brain processes the world, and you will see things in a different, more spiritual way. It may cause disruptions in an orderly life as you adjust to the inner change. Initiation is all about change at the core of who you are.

The rite provided is meant to supplement a candidate's preparation for initiation into a specific spiritual tradition or be used as part of a self-initiation ceremony. But realize that the spell here is done at the end of a period of learning, study, and dedication to a higher spiritual path. Many traditions demand at least a year and a day of study and preparation before an initiation can take place. We aren't saying you have to wait that long, but know that an initiation taken when the candidate is not properly prepared probably won't bring a useful effect.

The Symbols

We chose symbols that have been used for initiation throughout various cultures. If you have others, feel free to draw or paste them in for yourself.

Stairs going down into the earth—as in a Celtic long barrow (also known as a fairy mound, a place where the honored dead were buried) and also the entrance to a Native American sweat lodge (a warm, damp, womb-like space where sacred visions are sought)—are the path to the underworld, where initiation takes place.

Yggdrasil is the world tree. It is the central axis, the center point, on which the universe revolves. The roots of the tree enfold the underworld and the well of memory, the trunk is at Middelheim (the world where we live), and the branches and leaves are in the upper world (of Asgard and the gods).

The labyrinth symbolizes the path each of us walks as we journey through this life. It is full of unexpected twists and turns. It often feels like you are making no progress when actually you've come a long way. Labyrinthine journeys are used in many initiation rites throughout the world.

The person at the center is you, the initiate, going through a change, an ordeal.

Think of the "sacrifice" card from the tarot (Key XII). What are you willing to endure in order for Spirit to send you a priceless gift? Odin, the Norse shaman god and All-Father, has only one eye because he gave the other in a sacrifice to gain knowledge and wisdom. He hung upside-down on Yggdrasil for nine days and nights without food or drink, and the Norns gave him knowledge of the runes in exchange for his sacrifice and initiation.

Crescent moons with handprints symbolize Grandmother Moon as the midwife of the new you, there to catch you if you fall in an unseen, loving hug.

Spirals are symbols of the goddess and also of the journey into and out of the unconscious. Many initiations are accomplished in the mind, a journey of spirit into and back from the inner worlds, often bringing back new ideas, knowledge, or inspiration.

More symbols of initiation are the pentagram of enlightenment; the ankh of death and rebirth; the astrological glyph for Pluto, the planet of personal transformation; and a bind rune symbolizing knowledge gained through sacrifice.

Ritual to Prepare for Initiation

Suggested Colors
Purple is a color of deep secrets and mysteries.

Indigo is a color of the unconscious.

Green and blue are colors of safety.

Red, orange, and yellow are colors of energy, will, and determination.

Brown is a color of grounding and the depths.

Black is the color of the abyss to be crossed by the initiate so that they may attain what they seek and more.

Special Supplies
- a soft cloth to tie around your eyes for a blindfold
- a black candle
- a white candle

To Work This Spell
Recall the events that have brought you to this ritual. Think back on your life path's twists and turns that have brought you to where you are. Remember the events—good and bad—that have guided you and steeled your determination to take this step. Bless and thank those who have helped and guided you in your studies. Bless and thank those—even those who have harmed you—who have made you the person you are at present. Sometimes adversity is the best teacher.

Every initiation is different. Every tradition does it differently. We cannot give you words for your initiation, but we thought we would share an invocation you might use:

> All-Father Odin, you hung on the tree;
> none gave you food, none gave you drink.
> Your ordeal is legendary,
> yet you persevered and won the prize.
> You sacrificed an eye and gained so much more:
> hard-won knowledge,
> hard-won wisdom,
> hard-won strength.
> Let my initiation bring me gifts
> and let my sacrifice be worth the prize.
> All-Father Odin, guide me through the ordeal
> and let me come out stronger, better, more wise.

Light the black and white candles and place them to either side of you as you work your spell.

Invite Odin (or other deities of your choice) to guide you on your initiatory journey.

Color and decorate the Initiation page as you concentrate upon the knowledge and experience you are hoping to gain.

Write your personal affirmation in the box at the bottom of the page. Say the affirmation out loud three times (or chant it, sing it, or shout it multiple times) to empower the spell.

Tie the cloth around your eyes to block out the light.

Sit quietly and visualize yourself descending into the earth, walking down the stairs, going deeper and deeper until you cannot see the light above.

Settle yourself quietly in the darkness of the depths of the earth, and allow yourself to receive whatever the gods will give you. Take as much or as little time as you need.

Once you have received your gift, take a few moments and review the experience. Think back on your inner journey and cement it in your mind.

Take a deep, cleansing breath, and make your way back up into the world. See the light at the top of the stairs, and climb back into your day-to-day life.

Once you are back in the world, remove the blindfold and sit quietly, absorbing your experience. Then repeat your affirmation three times and reflect on how you may have changed.

Thank Odin and whatever other deities or elements you have called upon for attending on your behalf.

Close your circle and relax. Understand that it will be some time before you fully assimilate your initiatory experience.

Display your art somewhere appropriate to remind you of your initiation, and reflect upon the changes it has brought into your life.

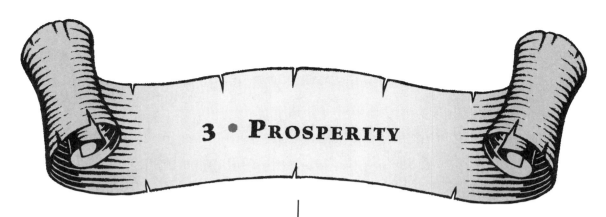

3 • PROSPERITY

PROSPERITY: the state of having enough for your needs with a bit left over for the things you might want but do not require for living.

The trick is to determine just how much is "enough plus a little more." As we get older, our needs change and mature. Our income may increase, but sometimes we don't appreciate just what is necessary and what is extra.

Think back and determine just what is vital for your living and what then becomes extra. Do you have any savings built up? True prosperity includes not living beyond your means, having a comfortable cushion in case of emergencies, and yet having enough for a few nice extras in your life. It's a balance.

The Symbols
We chose symbols that have been used for prosperity throughout various cultures. If you have others, feel free to draw or paste them in for yourself.

We used the astrological glyph for Taurus, which is the sign of abundance, fertility, physical comforts, and material possessions. Along the edges of the glyph are the phases of the moon, symbolizing the passage of time to bring forth a bountiful harvest.

A yin-yang symbol is used, representing a balance of light and dark, male and female, and hot and cold energies that remind us how all the resources of this world should be used wisely, in balance with our natural environment. One half of the yin-yang symbol contains a bright sun ripening a field of golden grain, representing harvest and abundance. The other half of the yin-yang symbol contains a cornucopia, also known as "the horn of plenty." The Italian goddess Fortuna, whose name means "fortune," was often depicted as holding a cornucopia with a shower of golden coins pouring forth to bless those on whom her favor rested.

Look for several Norse bind runes used as sigils of wealth, prosperity, home, and harvest.

Other symbols of prosperity are four golden coins (four being the number of the physical/material plane), gems, jewels, checks, dollars, coins, treasures, bank savings, and a snug little house.

Ritual for Prosperity

Suggested Colors
Green is a color of prosperity, fertility, and the ability to bring in the green stuff—money!

Gold and silver are colors of wealth.

Brown symbolizes the fertility of the earth and the bounty it can bring.

Red is the color of courage and action.

Yellow and orange are colors of ideas that can be used to generate income for security.

Special Supplies
- pictures or symbols of what you think prosperity means
- bills and bank statements that you can use as a focus for working on your personal prosperity
- pictures of money, security, wealth, and prosperity
- a green candle
- a gold candle

To Work This Spell

Light the two candles and invite Fortuna to shower you with her bounty.

Color and decorate the Prosperity page.

Here is a chant that has been effective in bringing money into a person's life:

> *Goddess, grant me enough—*
> *enough and a bit more*
> *wealth to keep me secure.*

Chant it loud and proud—chant it many times, knowing the energies you are sending out will bring opportunities to bring money to you.

Alternatively, you can call on the goddess Fortuna:

> *Fortuna, holder of the sacred cornucopia,*
> *grant me your bounty—*
> *bounty of money*
> *bounty of resources*
> *bounty of wealth*
> *bounty enough to share.*
> *Let your bounty make my life*
> *safe and comfortable.*

Write your personal affirmation in the box at the bottom of the page.

Say the affirmation out loud four times (or chant it, sing it, or shout it multiple times) to empower the spell.

Look at the bank statements and bills. Visualize the bank statements showing a good balance, savings, and a nice margin for extras. See the bills as being paid in full and being able to pay them off as they come in without having to pay over time. Know that you can get prosperity in your life and a good handle on your financial situation.

When finished, thank Fortuna and whatever other deities or elements you have called upon for attending on your behalf.

Close your circle and relax, confident that you can gain prosperity and financial security over time.

Display your art somewhere you can see and appreciate it. Smile every time you look at it, knowing you are working toward true prosperity! Know you can be financially free and have a cushion for emergencies.

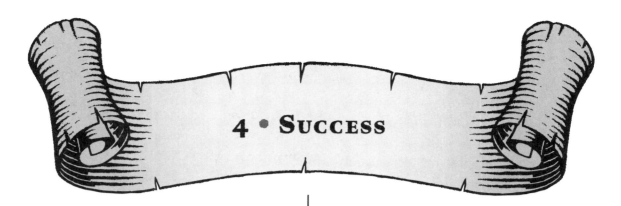

4 • SUCCESS

SUCCESS: the ability to make things go your way. To compete in the arena of life and come out on top, to win and have others see and acknowledge your achievements in a satisfying and meaningful way.

You *can* come out on top. You know what you need to do, and you have the will to keep at your task and practice so you can win when you are called on to perform or compete. Success comes one step at a time; you may have to work long hours, but eventually your efforts will pay off. You will come out on top—the winner, number one—and the world will acknowledge and celebrate your achievements!

Nike is the Greek goddess of victory. Her presence guaranteed those she favored would win and come out on top. Asking her to help you in your efforts and smile on your accomplishments will guarantee success in your endeavors. She will hand you the laurel wreath, symbolizing victory. She is winged and can move swiftly to crown you the winner at the moment of your triumph. Hear the cheers of the crowd as you stand before them crowned in your triumph!

The Symbols

We chose symbols that have been used for success throughout various cultures. If you have others, feel free to draw or paste them in for yourself.

We have used a trophy known as a "loving cup," a first-place prize in the shape of a chalice, Holy Grail, or cauldron of rebirth. From the cup is pouring forth a fountain of blessings in the form of water, fire, and spirit.

On the front of the trophy is a first-place blue ribbon given to the winner of a contest or competition.

In ancient Greece a wreath of laurel foliage was worn on the head as an emblem of victory. In ancient Rome a gilded laurel wreath became the crown of emperors. Here it crowns your achievement.

In ancient Greece a great festival was held every four years near the base of Mount Olympus, home of Zeus and the other Greek gods. Foot races and other athletic competitions gave the winners extreme honor. The Olympic torch is still lit from Olympia, Greece, by ten women "priestesses" before it is passed by foot relay over thousands of miles to the opening ceremonies of each of the international games.

Fancy filigree is often found on diplomas and other award certificates and indicates success.

Find Sowilo, the rune for victory.

Look for the astrological glyph for Jupiter (Roman version of Zeus, patron deity of the Olympics).

We also chose a thumbs-up sign and a crown to signify mastery or rulership.

Ritual for Success

Suggested Colors

Blue is the color of the winner's ribbon—first place!

Gold is the color of the trophy and gilded laurel symbolizing the accomplishment.

Green is the color of the laurel, the wreath of the victor.

Red is the color of courage and action.

Yellow is the color of ideas and the will to keep going.

Orange is a color of creativity for new and different ways to be a success.

Special Supplies

- pictures, mementos, or bits of paper from the area of life where you are looking for success

- a blue candle

- a green candle

- a gold candle

To Work This Spell

Light the blue candle and invite Nike to give you strength, inspiration, will, and success.

One possible Nike invocation is:

Winged Victory, Nike, goddess of victory,
she who blesses and reveals the winning side;
those whom she chooses will be crowned as the victors.
Success follows in her wake.
She grants the will and skill to come out on top.
Her eyes see the winners.
She shows the world those who are successful.
She will come and crown me!
Hail Nike, winged victory!

Light the green candle and ask Nike for the will and determination to keep at your task so you can be successful in the end.

Color and decorate the Success page. Pay close attention to each element: the loving cup; the blue ribbon; the laurel wreath; the rays of fire, water, and spirit; the symbols of success; the fancy border; the Olympic torch. Understand what you need to do to be a success; how you need to train and practice and work at your goal. Know that with your determination and your will, you can be a success and come out on top.

Write your personal affirmation in the box at the bottom of the page.

Say the affirmation out loud three times (or chant it, sing it, or shout it multiple times) to empower the spell.

Light the gold candle and repeat the Nike invocation.

Hold and admire the symbols of your success. Hear the applause and the cheers of the crowd as you receive the symbols of your success.

When finished, thank Nike and whatever other deities or elements you have called upon for attending on your behalf.

Close your circle and relax, confident that you will succeed in your endeavors.

Display your art somewhere you can see and appreciate it. Feel proud of your accomplishment and hear the cheers of the crowd as you are crowned the victor.

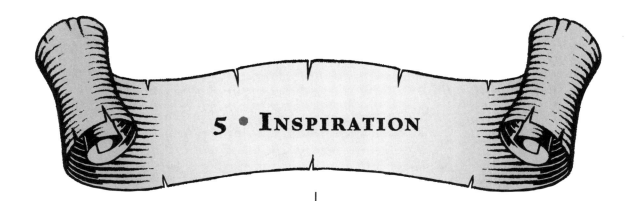

5 • INSPIRATION

INSPIRATION: the ability to see connections and form ideas about what already exists, then create new possibilities for growth, prosperity, right action, practical living, and learning.

Inspiration is to gain wisdom and understanding about one's self, the environment, life, the universe, the cosmos and beyond, psychic intuition and belief, and the gods and their realms. It is to be open to new ideas, new information, new techniques and skills, new ways of thinking and living, and new people in your life who can open new worlds to you.

The Muses are Greek goddesses who personify Inspiration in many guises and areas. They are either the daughters of Gaea and Ouranos or Zeus and Mnemosyne. They number three, four, or nine, depending on the sources. How many they are is not the point; they give inspiration to humankind, and calling on their help aids in creativity, gaining the ideas and drive to create new things.

The Symbols

We chose symbols that have been used for inspiration throughout various cultures. If you have others, feel free to draw or paste them in for yourself.

The cauldron of inspiration—from whence you drink deep to gain ideas and the knowledge and skills to make those ideas manifest. The tendrils of steam arise, and often just inhaling the vapors is enough to give good thoughts and ideas. They rise to heaven, showing how thoughts can carry us to wherever we can imagine.

The wings at the sides are the thoughts that wing their way to becoming real creations in the world.

The eye of wisdom decorates the cup, showing that divine influence often helps aid the seeker of wisdom.

The spiral of the Goddess can take you down into your subconscious and bring you back with the knowledge you seek.

The symbols of waxing and waning moons show that the moon is a guardian of memory, which also can help in bringing new thoughts. It also shows the time it can take to go from meditation to idea to thoughts of action to real action and then to completion for making those ideas and thoughts manifest in the world.

The rays around the circle are the rays of thought winging outward to become manifest.

Roots of desire and action—though thoughts are helpful, they must be accompanied with real action to manifest what we desire.

Braided lines symbolize the need for thought, understanding, and action to blend and create something new and useful.

Look for the astrological symbol of Pisces and the astrological symbol of Neptune, planetary ruler of Pisces. These rule the subconscious and wells of inspiration.

Find the star with a heart, showing how desire and love can make most anything manifest.

Look for the rune Ken, which indicates inspiration, mind, and thought.

Ritual for Inspiration

Suggested Colors

Blue is the color of mind and memory.

Green is the color of fertility.

Indigo symbolizes the deep mind and subconscious.

Yellow, orange, and red are the colors of action and energy to accomplish what you imagine.

Brown is a color of fertility and possibility for growth.

Special Supplies

- symbols or pictures of the sources of inspiration that work for you

- a blank page of paper or a notebook and a pen to write down any ideas that come to you as you work your spell

- a cup with a sweet beverage to drink from to fuel your mind for generating ideas

To Work This Spell

Light the candle and invite the Muses to come and inspire you for your stated purpose. Here is a sample invocation for the Muses:

Goddesses of mind and inspiration,
daughters of Gaea and Ouranos
(or daughters of Zeus and Mnemosyne),
students of Apollo divine, may the Muses
come to me and aid me in my purpose.
May they bring me ideas and the will and
energy to make manifest my ideas.
May I have the personal will and
purpose to complete my project.
May my project bring _____
for me and the world.

Color and decorate the Inspiration page.

Write your personal affirmation in the box at the bottom of the page.

Say the affirmation out loud three or nine times (or chant it, sing it, or shout it multiple times) to empower the spell.

Repeat the Muses' invocation.

Drink deep from your personal cup of inspiration, realizing that you are drinking in new ideas and thoughts.

Relax and let the ideas flow. Write them on the blank paper—do not censor or overthink. Just write whatever comes to you and be as open as you can be to whatever comes.

When finished, thank the Muses and whatever other deities or elements you have called upon for attending on your behalf.

Close your circle and relax, knowing that you are a person with many ideas and the will to make them manifest.

Display your art somewhere you can see and appreciate it. Have a pad of paper and a pen nearby to write down any additional ideas you might get when looking at it. Know that it is a portrait of the many and varied ideas you generate—a vessel of your will to make them come to life.

INSPIRATION

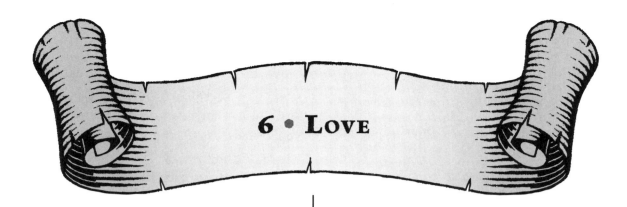

6 • LOVE

LOVE: the ability to put the needs of another over your own.

To love is to blend your life with another in every way in order to create a new being made up of the two of you, stronger and more complete than either of you can be alone. Love is feeling romance, desire, passion, and the need to be with the other. With love, sorrows can be halved and joys doubled.

The Symbols

We chose symbols that have been used for love throughout various cultures. If you have others, feel free to draw or paste them in for yourself.

A distlefink is the Pennsylvania Dutch goldfinch, a little bird of happiness.

A heart-shaped tree grows roses, the traditional flower of love and the alchemical symbol of feminine power and transcendence. To win love, you must be willing to get scratched by a few thorns along the way.

The tree is growing out of the sea of love, the subconscious mind where emotions originate. Also the cosmic ocean, where all separate and lonely beings are merged with deity into one divine unity.

A sunburst radiates light, warmth, and love from the heart center outward.

Look for the astrological glyph of Venus, the planet ruling love, art, and beauty, and the astrological symbol for Libra, the sign of balance, harmony, and partnerships. Libra is an auspicious sign to be married under, though there are others that work well also.

Find the X's, which are the runic symbol for Gifu, the rune of sharing, and the O's, which are a stylized symbol for Ing, the rune of Ingvy-Frey, a Norse/Germanic god of sex, fertility, and abundance. Together, the X's and O's are often written in love letters to symbolize hugs and kisses.

The hearts are there as a reminder that love comes from the fourth chakra, and to receive love you must first open up your heart center to giving love.

Ritual for Love

Suggested Colors

Red is the color of passion and action.

Pink is a color of affection and romance.

Blue is the color of the unconscious from whence attraction starts.

Yellow is a color of enthusiasm and energy.

In floriography, the Victorian flower language, various colors of roses had varied meanings. Here are a few:

White—beauty, purity, innocence, eternal love; I am worthy of you

Red—passion; I love you

Burgundy—unconscious beauty

Pink—perfect happiness, friendship, secret love; please believe me

Orange/coral—desire, passion, fascination

Yellow—joy, friendship, devotion, try to care, forgive and forget

Peach—immortality, modesty

Lavender/violet—enchantment, love at first sight

Blue—mystery, love at first sight, attaining the impossible

Red and white together—unity

Red and yellow together—joy, happiness, and excitement

Special Supplies

- a red candle

- a white candle

- a yellow candle

To Work This Spell

Light the red, white, and yellow candles. Invite Venus to make you ready to receive love into your life. One possible Venus invocation is:

Beautiful Venus, bringer of love and romance,
make me ready to give and receive love.
Let me be open to the possibility for
love, wherever it may come.
Help me to be worthy to love and be loved by another.
Help me to work at a loving relationship.
Help me weather the changes and challenges love brings.
Help me to have a loving, balanced, and healthy
partnership that stands the test of time.
Beautiful Venus, bring love into my life!

Color and decorate the Love page.

As you color your page, think of all the places you could meet someone. As you plan to get out and circulate, think about how you will dress and act. Visualize your friends introducing you to someone new. Be open to meeting new people. Think about what you have to offer someone to make their life better and what you can contribute to a loving relationship.

Write your personal affirmation in the box at the bottom of the page. Say the affirmation out loud six times (or chant it, sing it, or shout it multiple times) to empower the spell. Six is a sacred number of Venus.

Send your loving energy out into the universe and know it will find that special person for you. Understand that love is a process and may take some time, but know you will attain love if you are patient and true to your purpose.

When finished, thank Venus and whatever other deities or elements you have called upon for attending on your behalf.

Close your circle and relax, knowing that love will come into your life.

Display your art somewhere you can see and appreciate it. Feel the warm rush of love when you see it, and know that special someone is out there waiting for you.

7 • SAFE TRAVEL

SAFE TRAVEL: getting from place to place in safety with the confidence that you will be secure.

Travel can be an adventure, but the actual getting from place to place should be safe and secure. Hone your ability to be alert and aware of conditions and of others traveling alongside you, and cultivate the skill of navigating whatever paths you follow to get to your destination.

The Symbols

We chose symbols that symbolize travel throughout the world. If you have others, feel free to draw or paste them in for yourself.

The broom is a symbolic vehicle you can imagine whatever you use in your travels. The luggage and animal carrier are for the baggage and companions you might choose to accompany you on your way. The rider is wearing a helmet, pads, heavy boots, and appropriate clothing. You will be protected however you choose to travel.

The waxing crescent moon and stars show the imagination and exploration that travel can create. A waxing moon makes for a good journey.

The silhouette of forest and city shows that you can travel wherever you want—there are no limitations to your wanderings.

Maps are for the places you might travel to, turning the symbols on the map into the reality of being there. Using a map, you can plan your journey without getting lost.

Look for the compass rose, showing you can travel in any direction.

Find the rune Raidho, symbolizing travel and safe journeying.

The astrological symbol for Sagittarius denotes long-distance travel and encountering foreign cultures and people.

A passport allows you to travel anywhere in the world; it is your ticket to new and different places.

Ritual for Safe Travel

Suggested Colors

Yellow and orange are colors of curiosity, enthusiasm, and excitement.

Blue is a color of calm and of water that you cross as you travel.

Brown and green are colors of earth and of growing things that you might see on your travels.

Violet is a color of mysteries that you may encounter in your travels.

Pink is a color of warm, happy memories that you are creating as you travel.

Special Supplies

• a white candle

• a silver candle

To Work This Spell

Light the white and silver candles and invite Hermes, god of travelers, to guide and protect you on your journey.

One possible Hermes invocation is:

> *Hermes the Traveler, god of the road,*
> *guide and protect me as I journey.*
> *Give me your insight and understanding.*
> *Let me follow the paths in safety and comfort.*
> *Let me leave at a good time, travel well,*
> *and arrive whole and sound.*
> *Make my journey pleasant and instructive,*
> *safe and reliable, swift and steady.*
> *Allow me to arrive at my destination*
> *hale and whole and healthy.*
> *Hermes the Traveler, be my travel companion.*

Color and decorate the Safe Travel page.

As you color your page, think of all the places you want to travel to. Even the far-off fantasy vacations are possible with work and application. If you have a specific destination in mind, find pictures of that place and paste them onto the Safe Travel page. Visualize yourself in that place having a good time.

Write your personal affirmation in the box at the bottom of the page. Say the affirmation out loud three times (or chant it, sing it, or shout it multiple times) to empower the spell.

Send your safe travel energy out into the universe and know it will make your journey safe, secure, and easy.

When finished, thank Hermes and whatever other deities or elements you have called upon for attending on your behalf.

Here is a possible dismissal for Hermes:

> *Hermes the Traveler, god of the road,*
> *thank you for your guidance and protection.*
> *Thank you for your insight and understanding.*
> *Thank you for allowing me to follow*
> *the paths in safety and comfort.*
> *Thank you for allowing me to leave at a good time,*
> *travel well, and arrive whole and sound.*
> *Thank you for making my journey pleasant and*
> *instructive, safe and reliable, swift and steady.*
> *Allow me to arrive at my destination*
> *hale and whole and healthy.*
> *Hermes the Traveler, thank you for*
> *being my travel companion.*

Close your circle and relax, knowing that you will have safe travel.

Display your art somewhere you can see and appreciate it. Feel the excitement of pending travel when you see it, and know that you will have a good trip.

8 • STRENGTH

STRENGTH: the ability to accomplish what you need to do. It can be physical strength for physical tasks, emotional strength for difficult times that need to be worked through, or spiritual strength for those times when you know what is right but difficult to do. Strength allows us to act effectively and do what needs to be done.

There are many types of strength, and this image shows them.

The Symbols

We chose symbols that have been used for strength throughout various cultures. If you have others, feel free to draw or paste them in for yourself.

The shield and weapons show what is needed for a physical contest. They are ready for use, but if you don't have to use them, so much the better. The shield has a sun wheel of dragons with the rune Sowilo in the center. Sowilo is a rune of the sun and symbolizes the strength and endurance to accomplish our task. It is also a rune of victory and the feeling of accomplishment when you manage your task. The sun is steadfast and steady; her light brings life to the planet.

The Valkyrie helm can protect us while we act, and the one gleam calls to mind their father, one-eyed Odin the All-Father. The wings on the helmet show thoughts that are necessary to act properly and use strength effectively. The Valkyries, goddesses of Fate, chose who would win and lose in battle.

Below are a mother bear and cub. There is a great deal of strength in the mother bear, who will fight for her offspring.

The other animal is an aurochs, a giant ox that lived in earlier times in Europe but has been hunted to extinction. The aurochs was immensely powerful, with horns many feet in length. The aurochs shows male strength. Find the rune Ur, which symbolizes the aurochs and is a rune of massive strength that needs to be controlled.

The redwood trees, known for their grandeur and strength, show that trees provide shelter.

The rune Thurisaz is another rune of strength and power.

The astrological sign of Taurus the bull is a sign of the immovable force, fixed earth. When Taurus digs in their heels, it takes a great deal to make them budge. Taurus is strong and steadfast.

The astrological sign for Mars shows the energy and power necessary to act with strength. Just be sure to act appropriately and with good thought beforehand.

Ritual for Strength

Suggested Colors
Yellow and orange are colors of the sun and light.

Red is the color of raw power, which can be controlled.

Brown and green are colors of earth and growing things, which are steadfast and strong.

Blue is the color of calm and control.

Black is a color of intensity and fortitude.

Purple is a color of deep mysteries from where the knowledge to properly use your strength can come.

Special Supplies
- a red candle
- a yellow or gold candle

To Work This Spell

Light the red and yellow candles and invite Sunna, goddess of the sun, to grant you the strength you need. One possible Sunna invocation is:

> Sunna, sun goddess,
> bright bride of heaven, weaver of light,
> healer and maker of the music of the spheres.
> Grant me strength that I may accomplish my purpose.
> Allow me to feel your healing energies
> and make me strong—
> strong in mind,
> strong in heart,
> strong in body.
> Help me to use my strength well and wisely
> so I can do what needs to be done
> and be effective and successful in my purpose.
> Sunna, sun goddess, I call on your strength.

Color and decorate the Strength page.

As you color your page think about the purpose you have that you need the strength for. What is it you mean to accomplish? How will you go about it? What resources do you need? Visualize yourself getting what you need and doing what you need to do. Visualize yourself as a strong and effective person, confident and assured you can manage the task, whatever it may be.

Write your personal affirmation in the box at the bottom of the page. Say the affirmation out loud nine times (or chant it, sing it, or shout it multiple times) to empower the spell.

Send your energy out into the universe and know you will be granted the strength to accomplish your task.

When finished, thank Sunna and whatever other deities or elements you have called upon for attending on your behalf.

Here is a possible dismissal for Sunna:

> Sunna, goddess of the sun,
> bright bride of heaven, weaver of light,
> healer and maker of the music of the spheres.
> I thank you for your guidance and energy.
> I thank you for the strength you have given me—
> strength of mind,
> strength of heart,
> strength of body.
> Help me to use my strength well and wisely,
> that I may accomplish my purpose.
> Grant me effective success in my purpose.
> I thank you Sunna, sun goddess.

Close your circle and relax, knowing that you will have the strength you need.

Display your art somewhere you can see and appreciate it. Feel the strength you have been granted when you see it, and know that you can use that strength whenever you need it.

9 • AUTONOMY

AUTONOMY: the state of being self-sufficient, needing nothing but your own counsel and ideas to make your way in the world, allowing you to open yourself to the universe and derive inspiration and enlightenment therefrom.

Sometimes we need to take a break from the regular world and fly among the clouds, free to imagine whatever we wish. Other people can hold you back, and you occasionally need to get away by yourself and discover just exactly who you are and what you are about.

Once you are floating in the clouds, you can look around, see things from a higher perspective, and maybe gain some insights about life, the universe, and everything.

The Symbols

We chose symbols that have been used for autonomy throughout various cultures. If you have others, feel free to draw or paste them in for yourself.

A woman sitting in the lotus position on an actual lotus flower is peaceful and inwardly directed, meditating deeply. She wears a necklace of beads, symbolizing the days and steps necessary to attain enlightenment and inner peace. The necklace is the circle of life and reincarnation as well.

A design that may be the sun, may be decoration, or may be something the woman dreamed up in her imagination, shows there are no limits to how you can attain autonomy. Whatever it is, it came from her mind and is hers alone.

Clouds of imagination, thought, and mental concentration show she is floating in the clouds

and free of the constraints of the material world. In our mind we can be and do anything we can imagine. There are no limits to the mind.

Designs from the imagination show autonomy in thought. Beautiful and intricate, they may not be real, but they are meaningful and inspiring nonetheless.

Look for the astrological symbol for the sun, the planet of personal autonomy and sense of self.

Find the rune Ken, symbolizing bringing light into dark places, inspiration, mind/ thought, understanding, ideas, and inner guidance.

The peace symbol was created to symbolize peace, tranquility, and inner understanding.

The symbol for the Hindu word *om* shows the sound made by the world breathing. Chanting *om* can bring inner peace.

Ritual for Autonomy

Suggested Colors

Green is the color of health, money, and abundance.

Silver and gold are the colors of money and wealth.

Yellow is the color of intellect and right action.

Brown is the color of the earth and wood, symbols of material things.

Blue is the color of a clear, calm mind that is open to new possibilities.

A rainbow has all colors, showing all the possibilities of life.

Special Supplies
- a blue candle (symbolizing a calm, clear mind)
- a white candle (symbolizing all the possibilities in life)

To Work This Spell

Clear your mind and relax. Allow yourself to become open to what the universe has to offer you. Realize you need to keep an open mind so you can take advantage of the ideas and opportunities that present themselves to you.

Light your candles and invite Athena into your circle, and perhaps use them as a focus for meditation.

Grey-eyed Athena, goddess of mind
and clear, considered thought,
you who sprang fully grown and
armed from the head of Zeus,
virgin goddess who needs no consort or partner,
help me to gain autonomy.
Help me to see how I can rely upon my own resources.
Help me to be self-sufficient and centered.
Help me to help myself be independent.

Take time to color your picture spell. Also take time for meditation and consideration as you color.

Write your personal affirmation at the bottom.

When you have finished, thank Athena.

Grey-eyed Athena, virgin goddess,
autonomous and independent,
thank you for your insights.
Thank you for showing me
how I can be independent,
how I can be self-sufficient and centered,
how I can rely upon my own resources.
Thank you for granting me autonomy.
Help me to keep my independence and
self-reliance as I make my way through life.
Thank you for showing me the way.

Thank whatever deities or elements you have called upon for attending on your behalf.

Close your circle and relax, knowing you are on your way toward autonomy and independence. Know you can work on that and enjoy a fulfilling life.

Display your art somewhere appropriate as a reminder of your autonomy and how you are self-reliant and self-assured.

AUTONOMY

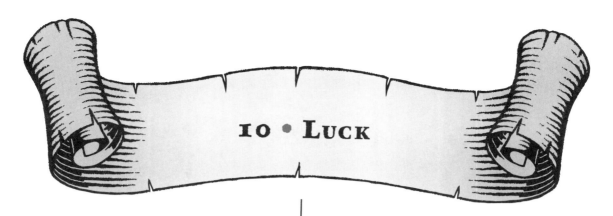

LUCK: good fortune, abundance, fortunate happenings, taking advantage of a situation or resources.

Luck is sometimes seen as something outside ourselves, something that we get or don't get, yet for many luck is the ability to see possibilities and make the most of circumstances. So in many ways we make our own luck by staying alert, recognizing the possibilities in circumstances good or bad, and taking advantage of whatever resources are at hand.

When you do the ritual, realize that maybe luck can just happen and maybe you can make your own luck by taking advantage of whatever life brings you. Be open to both kinds of luck, and don't limit yourself by expecting a specific lucky thing to happen. There are many more kinds of luck than just winning the lottery—and if you want to win the lottery, remember you need to buy a ticket or you will never win.

The Symbols

We chose symbols that have been used for luck throughout various cultures. If you have others, feel free to draw or paste them in for yourself.

A horseshoe with ends pointed upward is used to catch luck.

A ship's wheel is used to steer the ship to a safe harbor for sailors and travelers in general. The wheel has eight spokes, symbolizing the wheel of the year; the area between the spokes corresponds to each of the eight sabbats. The eight spokes are at each quarter and cross-quarter, and also symbolize the eight paths to the center of your being. Like a fruitful harvest, your luck can come in good time. You can ride the wheel from any place—at the top or the bottom, rising or falling. The wheel goes round and round, and luck is always in motion.

A rabbit's foot is a lucky charm. A rainbow is a symbol of hope and a better future; the clouds with rain show that even rainclouds have a silver lining. Fair weather is a good luck omen. Cornucopias (horns of plenty) and four-leaved clovers are traditional symbols of good luck, as are lucky pennies, wishbones, and dice showing the lucky number 7.

Look for the astrological symbols for Jupiter (the planet of greater fortune, abundance, and good luck) and Venus (the planet of lesser fortune, luck, and pleasant times). Find the runes Jera (harvest, representing the good things which come after hard work and right actions) and Pertho (the dice cup, denoting good chance and lucky fortune).

Ritual for Luck

Suggested Colors

Green is the color of money and abundance.

Silver and gold are the colors of money and wealth.

Brown is the color of the earth and wood, symbols of material things.

Blue is the color of a clear, calm mind that is open to new possibilities.

A rainbow has all colors, showing all the possibilities of life.

Special Supplies

- a purple candle for Jupiter, the greater fortune

- a green candle for Venus, the lesser fortune

- pictures or symbols of what you think luck means

To Work This Spell

Light your purple and green candles, for the planets of the greater and lesser fortunes, Jupiter and Venus.

Call on the goddess Fortuna to help you gain good luck.

You can say something like:

Lady of the cornucopia,
she who guides the rudder of the fates.
Goddess Fortuna, bring me luck.
Grant me opportunities for making my
lot better, my life more fortunate.
Let me see what comes before me as
an opportunity for good,
an opportunity for advancement,
an opportunity for fortune.
Bring me all the good luck I can handle,
and allow me to use it to my best advantage.

Take time to color your picture spell.

Write your personal affirmation at the bottom.

When you have finished, thank the goddess Fortuna:

Dame Fortune, lady of the cornucopia,
guide of the rudder of fate, goddess Fortuna:
thank you for granting me luck
so I may better myself and my life.
Keep my eyes open to new opportunities
so I may take best advantage of what
the universe will bring to me.
Bless me with your fortunate gifts.

Thank whatever deities or elements you have called upon for attending on your behalf.

Close your circle and relax, confident that you can take advantage of the opportunities life will bring you so you can make your own good luck.

Display your art somewhere appropriate as a reminder of your luck and how you will see and use whatever opportunities come your way.

II · JUSTICE

JUSTICE: fair dealings; being just, fair, lawful, and reasonable; deserved reward or punishment; trial and judgment by law; gaining satisfaction after a loss or injury through lawful means.

Maat, implacable keeper of the scales, will someday weigh the worthiness of your soul and ask if your heart is lighter than a feather. If it is not, then think about what weighs you down. Do you feel guilt over something you've done or said? Are you angry over an injustice done to you? Perhaps it was an insult done to someone or something you care about? Has someone betrayed your trust?

Explore and express your possible rage, hurt, loss, and shame. Do some journaling on this issue. Visualize yourself taking pride in getting some "just rewards" in a way that brings no harm to others. In the case of a friend who was raped, we did this ritual to ask that the perpetrator be caught and imprisoned. Some people might consider this bringing harm to him, but we personally believe that preventing further rapes serves the greater good for all concerned. Please weigh all possible outcomes of your spellcraft with extreme care before proceeding. Take responsibility for the consequences that will occur.

Justitia, the goddess of justice, wears a blindfold. She is completely impartial. If you need to take your grievances to a proper authority, be sure that all of your facts are carefully documented and witnesses can corroborate your story. Be completely honest with everyone involved—especially yourself. Do you truly have good cause for righteous anger? Remember: Justitia's sword is double edged—it can cut both ways. The flower of revenge has many thorns. Let the winds of clear thinking blow free.

The Symbols

We chose symbols that have been used for justice throughout various cultures. If you have others, feel free to draw or paste them in for yourself.

The sword of justice, the Sword of Solomon, symbolizes that justice cuts both ways. The pentagram at the pommel shows all five elements are employed in attaining justice.

The owl is a symbol of Athena, the Greek goddess who advocated law and justice rather than the rule of the strongest.

The rose vine with its flowers and thorns shows that justice can be sweet but also have harsh consequences if we aren't careful how we go about attaining it.

The scales holding a heart and a feather symbolize Maat, the Egyptian goddess of law and justice. Her laws made the Egyptian society fair and peaceful through the rule of good and well-administered laws.

Lightning bolts of retribution are for those who defy the law and codes of right living.

The blindfolded goddess Justitia shows that the law is impartial and applies to all.

Clouds symbolize the element of air, the element of rationality and knowledge needed to administer proper justice, and the swiftness of the wind that can accompany justice making things whole again.

Look for the astrological symbols for the planet Saturn and sign of Libra. Saturn is the planet of society and its limitations and responsibilities. Libra is the sign of law and justice.

Find the runes Tiwaz (strength and honor) and Sowilo (victory).

Ritual Asking for Justice to Be Done

Suggested Colors

Red or pink for the heart (express your emotions around this issue), the roses (a happy outcome that makes you feel better about yourself), and Tiwaz (rune of strength and honor).

Yellow or gold for the lightning (swift and powerful action), the sunny sky (yellow symbolizing air and intellect), Sowilo (rune of victory), and Athena's golden hair.

Blue for Justitia's blindfold (that cooler heads may prevail) and the Libra glyph (for balance).

Black or dark gray for the Saturn glyph (for drawing boundaries and setting limits).

Special Supplies

- something symbolizing the issue at hand: a photo, a legal document, a small object, etc.

- a symbol of Athena: something with an owl, olives, a book, a small toy with a shield, helmet or spear are possible options

- a small amount of olive oil

- parchment or other clean sheet of paper and a fireproof receptacle to burn it in

- a white candle

To Work This Spell

Recall the events that have brought you to this ritual. Allow any and all negative emotions to come up (anger, hate, hurt, jealousy, rage, feeling victimized, guilt; whatever)—and write words or symbols upon your parchment in red to express these feelings. Have a good cry if you want. When you are done, put the parchment aside.

Take up the white candle and dress it with olive oil (sacred to Athena) by wiping a small amount over the sides. Put it in your candle holder.

Place your symbol of Athena before the candle, next to your symbol of the matter at hand.

Light the white candle and invite Athena to join you in your spell.

One possible invocation of Athena is:

> *Grey-eyed Athena, golden-haired goddess*
> *who brought law and justice to society,*
> *aid me in this endeavor to gain justice.*
> *Guide me in my efforts to make things right,*
> *to make whole and gain restitution.*
> *Help me to bring those who have done wrong to justice.*
> *Help me to bring their crimes to light.*
> *Help me to show how they have wronged me (or whoever).*
> *Help me to prove their guilt.*
> *Help me to make sure they are appropriately punished.*
> *Help me to see they pay their debt to me and society.*
> *Help me to heal and overcome this injustice done to me.*
> *Help me to find the peace of satisfaction.*
> *Athena, hold me under your aegis**
> *and keep me safe as justice is worked.*
> *Grey-eyed Athena, goddess of justice, aid me!*

Color and decorate the Justice page.

---

* Aegis: Athena's goat-skin shield; being under the aegis meant to be protected by Athena's power.

As you color the page, look at the symbols of the matter at hand. Ask that the perpetrators be discovered and brought to the law. Do not dwell exactly on how it will be done, but only that they meet their appropriate justice for their actions.

Write your personal affirmation in the box at the bottom of the page. Say the affirmation out loud three times (or chant it, sing it, or shout it) to empower the spell.

Take the parchment you have written on and tear it up into many small pieces. Place the pieces in the fireproof receptacle you have chosen to burn them. Use the flame of the candle to light the parchment on fire. Watch it burn. As all the pieces burn to ash, feel all your negative emotions burn away, leaving you calm and clear-headed so you can pursue your justice with a clear, rational mind.

Once the parchment is burned totally, let it cool. Stir the ash, then dispose of it in water—flushing it down the toilet works well.

When finished, thank Athena and whatever other deities or elements you have called upon for attending on your behalf.

Close your circle and relax, knowing justice will be done. It may take time, but the energies have been released and the wheels are turning to grant satisfaction in the fullness of time.

Display your art somewhere you can see and appreciate it. Every time you look at it, know that justice is being done and you will gain satisfaction and peace.

MEMORIAL: the process of saying goodbye to a departed loved one.

It is said that funerals are for the living and are a necessary part of the grieving and letting-go process that accompanies a death. Every society and culture has some sort of memorial ritual. Saying goodbye to the departed is part of being human. Allow yourself to feel and express your grief. Once you have done so, the healing can begin.

Permanent separations are painful and can be very lonely. This ritual is written for one person to do in private to honor the memory of a departed loved one, be they spouse, partner, friend, relative, or pet. It provides an opportunity to remember the specialness of a life now gone and perhaps communicate some love and blessings one more time. It is particularly appropriate to do this rite soon after a death or in late October or November at the dying time of the year or during the dark of the moon.

Isis was the great goddess of ancient Egypt. Her husband, Osiris, was slain and cut into pieces. She mourned and searched the world for his parts so that he could be properly buried and honored. Isis represents anyone who has lost a loved one. She guides and comforts the bereaved and shows them the way through their grief. She reminds us all that though the beloved may be gone, our life continues, and we can honor their memory by living a good life for ourselves.

The Symbols

We chose symbols that have been used for memorial and crossing over throughout various cultures. If you have others, feel free to draw or paste them in for yourself.

A skull symbolizes the mortality of all living beings. The skull has a light in one eye, showing that death kills only the body—the spirit still lives on.

A dark waning moon symbolizes the appropriate time for mourning and letting go.

The sea of the unconscious and also the waters of the river Styx are powerful symbols of death and the journey of the departed spirit. There is a boat with a ferryman who transports all souls from the land of the living to the halls of the dead.

A sun with flaming, fiery rays—is it setting or rising?

A dove of peace shows the peace of the grave and also is a symbol for the spirit that is eternal.

The skies symbolize heaven and various places where honored dead go to rest until they may return.

Snakes shed their skins and renew themselves. They also represent the wisdom to know that death is a part of life, as is birth, and everyone must experience both. Death is not the end, but merely a transition to another plane of existence.

More symbols of death and rebirth are the rune Dagaz (indicating the awakening that the transformation of death can bring), a sickle (showing all are cut down in time), a pomegranate (by which Persephone was required to dwell in Hades for part of every year), and an ankh (symbol of life, death, and rebirth).

Ritual for a Memorial, Funeral, or Rite of Crossing Over

Suggested Colors

White is the color of purity and also a bare skull. It is the color of mourning in the East.

Black is the color of death and the abyss, and also the color of mourning in Europe and the Americas.

Blue is the color of the skies, water, and calm.

Green is a color of life and resurrection.

Purple and indigo are the colors of mysteries, deep secrets, and the unconscious.

Red and gold are colors of the rising and setting sun and the spark of life within each of us.

Special Supplies

- photograph(s) of the deceased, color-copied for use in a collage so they can be cut up without damaging an original photograph

- scraps of paper with loved one's handwriting if available

- magazine photos that remind you of the deceased (vacation destinations, hobbies, etc.), including images of the paradise where they now dwell

- small tokens or toys representing the deceased's life (for example: a small plastic sailboat if they liked to sail, car keys, concert ticket stubs, old buttons from a favorite jacket, small symbols of their faith).

- dried rosebuds, rose petals, or other dried flowers

- black or white veil fabric

- scissors and glue

- optional fresh flowers

- a dinner setting of the deceased's favorite food and drink

- appropriate music

- 13 black or white candles

- 13 candle holders

To Work This Spell

Gather your supplies and prepare a clean, sacred area to set up a memorial shrine. This should be a place where you can leave it up for a while, as long as you want to.

Take some time to color and decorate the Memorial page.

Set up the memorial shrine, putting the art page in the center. Drape the veil fabric above the center of the art and down each side of the shrine.

Place the candles around and in front of the art; be careful to keep them away from anything that might catch fire!

Prepare the ritual meal. Make enough food to eat some and share some with the deceased.

Prepare the ritual toast. You can use an alcoholic beverage or something else. Use a special goblet for your toast.

Turn on the music and ask the deceased to come and be with you.

A possible invocation:

> *Great Isis, mother of Horus,*
> *widow of Osiris, be with me.*
> *Hold me in your loving embrace.*
> *Comfort me in my grief.*
> *Grant that I might commune with _____ one more time.*
> *I drink a toast in her/his loving memory.*
> *I dedicate this meal to you and my beloved.*
> *Share food with me and my beloved.*
> *Grant me solace and peace.*

Drink a toast; eat a portion of the meal, saving the rest for your loved one.

Talk to the deceased as if he or she is really standing there in front of you.

Allow your emotions to flow freely, expressing your grief in a healthy and cleansing way.

At the conclusion of the meal, give a blessing upon the departed's soul. You can say something like:

> Hella, beautiful and terrifying lady of Niffelheim,
> Persephone, queen of the underworld,
> Sophia, holy mother spirit,
> Isis, great mother:
> Please comfort and care for _____.
> May she/he be welcomed into
> the summerland of rest and plenty.
> May she/he be rejoined in happiness
> with loved ones who have journeyed on before,
> especially _____ (list names),
> and dwell in joy and peace
> until the next lifetime to come.
> So mote it be!

Thank whatever deities or elements you have called upon for attending on your behalf.

Display your ancestor shrine for thirteen hours, days, weeks, months, or for however long feels appropriate to you.

At the end of your ritual, after you have taken down the circle, you may take the uneaten portion of the meal and share it with the fairies or small creatures that inhabit the outdoors. Alternatively, you can eat it yourself, keeping in mind that this portion is for the person you are memorializing.

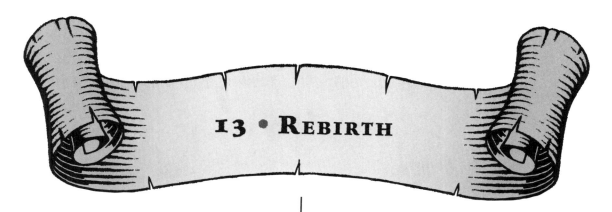

13 · Rebirth

REBIRTH: renewal, rejuvenation.

Sometimes we all need a change. Sometimes unwelcome changes are thrust upon us. Either way, it is a good thing to ritually mark transition points in life. It is important to regularly take the time to acknowledge that, in some small way, you are not the same person you used to be.

The ritual below is written for one person to do in private. It's particularly suited for a spring sabbat, a spring full moon, or any waxing moon. It could also work well as a lovely occasion for close friends or female family members to give a ritual bath for a female undergoing a transformation in her life: a girl upon reaching her womanhood; a bride on the morning of her wedding day; a woman going through a long labor before childbirth; a woman parted from a lover; or as part of a croning ritual at the end of the child-bearing years.

Feel free to adapt it as needed. The important thing is that the person the ritual is for feels pampered and empowered by the experience.

The Symbols

We chose symbols that have been used for rebirth throughout various cultures. If you have others, feel free to draw or paste them in for yourself.

The phoenix rising from the flames depicts rebirth. As such, she is her own mother over and over again through the ages. The flames arise from the death of her old self and are at once her funeral pyre and also the flames of her rebirth.

A blazing sun rising to give birth to a brand-new day year after year is a universal rebirth image.

An early springtime garden with tulips and pussy willows heralds the coming of warmer weather as the earth goddess rises from the underworld each spring to bless the earth with a fresh new growing season.

More rebirth symbols are dragonflies and butterflies as they dance in the warm breeze. Each butterfly is a miracle of nature, reborn from a chrysalis where a caterpillar transformed itself.

Look for the astrological symbol for Scorpio, a sign of sex, death, and rebirth. Scorpio is a unique sign in that it has three different animals that can represent it: a scorpion for the sign's lower vibrations, an eagle for the sign's middle vibrations, and the phoenix for the sign's higher vibrations.

Eggs are a powerful symbol of rebirth. We used an Ostara (Easter) egg, named for the goddess Ostara, an ancient Germanic earth goddess of the springtime whose name means "movement towards the rising sun." Eggs have obvious fertility implications, but each one also contains a small golden sun nestled within its shell (representing earth) ready to rise and give birth to a new day.

Look for the runes Pertho (fate and rebirth) and Dagaz (a new beginning, a new day is dawning).

Ritual for Rebirth

Suggested Colors

Purple is the color of spirit and the mysteries.

Red, orange, and yellow are the colors of fire, the sun, and the energy of re-creation.

Brown is the color of the earth and wood, symbols of this material world we live in.

Green is the color of growth and spring.

Special Supplies

- a black candle for the Crone, the destroyer
- a red candle for the Mother, the creatrix
- a white candle for the Maiden, she who is created
- a clean bathtub, soap, washcloths, sponges, scrubby brush, etc.
- bathroom mirror
- soothing, non-distracting music
- several large fluffy towels
- aromatherapy oils or bubble bath
- salt for cleansing (you can use scented bath salts)
- hair band (or other way of putting your hair up)
- a waterproof clear plastic sheet to hold your artwork in

To Work This Spell

Recall the events that have brought you to this ritual. Think about what needs changing in your life and the person you want to become. Know that seeing what you want is the first step to achieving it.

Light the black candle for the Crone—for the old life you are leaving behind.

Say something like:

> Dark mother, destroyer, ancient one of
> wisdom and mystery, be with me now.
> I sacrifice my old self for you to devour.
> May the compost of my life provide fertile ground
> on which to build a new beginning.

Secure your hair out of the way. Look at yourself in the mirror. See the former "you" being left behind.

Turn on the music and take time to color your picture spell.

Place the art in the plastic waterproof sleeve. Display it so that you can easily view it while soaking in the tub.

Run some warm water in the tub.

Strip off your clothes.

Get wet, and use the salt to scrub away old energies and purify yourself for the new energies you bring into yourself. You don't need a lot, just enough to feel the grit of the salt as you wipe it along your body.

Look at yourself in the mirror. Do not be critical of your body; revel in its beauty! Thank the gods and goddesses for the gift of life that each movement, each breath, each thought brings. Your body is your instrument of power; it is a blessing!

Light the red candle for the Mother and ask her to give birth to a new you.

Say something like:

> Bountiful mother, beautiful lady;
> fertile giver of life and all its pleasures,
> be with me now.
> I surrender up my fear
> to make room in my heart
> for your infinite love.
> Let your presence wash over me.

Add the oils to the tub, adding enough water to bring the whole thing to perfection.

Get in and have a good soak. Look at your art and take time to meditate.

When you feel renewed, get out of the tub and wrap up in some warm towels.

Light the white candle for the Maiden; feel her youthful vibrancy and strength. You can say something like:

> Vibrant maiden, steadfast warrior,
> eternal youth of strength and innocence,
> be with me now.
> I am ready to take up the challenges before me.
> May the promise of this new dawn be my
> guiding beacon in the days to come!

Thank whatever deities or elements you have called upon for attending on your behalf.

Close your circle and relax, confident that you are making a good start on the first day of the rest of your life.

Display your art somewhere appropriate as a reminder of your true inner beauty and the transformation you have undergone.

14 • FRIENDSHIP

FRIENDSHIP: the basis of individual happiness and societal units.

Friends are the people you like, in spite of their faults and your differences. Friends make experiences better by sharing them. They can help you in times of need or sorrow, and you help them as they need it.

True friendship is a reciprocal relationship, each doing as they can and helping when they are needed, and then deriving joy, companionship, and comradeship from the friendship. With shared interests and activities, friendships grow closer and deeper with the passage of time. We all need friends.

The Norse god Baldur the Bright was well-beloved and a friend to all. You might want to call him to witness and aid your rite.

The Symbols

We chose symbols that have been used for friendship throughout various cultures. If you have others, feel free to draw or paste them in for yourself.

Two interconnected gold rings represent two separate individuals joining together. The center of the overlapped rings forms a vesica piscis, a yoni-shaped band that represents the divine eminence of the Goddess. Note the room for names here at the cosmic center.

Each ring also contains a water lily/lotus blossom, a Buddhist symbol of self-creation and the sacred life force. Note that each flower is a unique self-contained element arising from different world-views in opposite directions, yet together they are in harmony and balance.

Two fish swimming in opposite directions represent the astrological sign of Pisces, the sign of the zodiac most associated with heart-felt sensitivity, charity, and wanting to do good for others. True friendship means wanting to put the welfare of another before your own—not because of obligation or duty but rather out of a need to share love.

Binding it all together is a braided cord, much like those used to weave friendship bracelets or handfasting cords. Separate strands are woven together to make a stronger new single entity.

The waters of the unconscious, the primal ocean we are each born from, our tides of emotion, show that it is at this level that true friends first connect.

Carved pillars of stone are solid, enduring, and permanent. They support great monuments of art and culture.

Other friendship symbols are hearts joined together, a yin-yang symbol of balance, and a Gifu rune of sharing.

Ritual of Friendship

The rite provided here is meant to be done together by two people as a way of acknowledging how much they mean to each other, cementing their relationship in a sort of formal way. Romantic partners or just good friends can do this. Alternatively, this ritual can be modified for one person who is looking to bring new friends into her or his life.

Suggested Colors

Pink is for matters of the heart, especially self-love, and friendship.

Yellow is also a good color for friendship and vibrant energy.

Gold for the rings, wealth, and commitment.

Blue for the waters of unconsciousness above and below.

Green for the lotus stems and leaves is a very healing color, and it also pertains to matters of the heart.

Other colors as they feel appropriate—the columns could be colored for the seven colors of the rainbow, one for each chakra, for example.

Special Supplies

- a lock of each person's hair (use someone else's hair only with permission) or 3 lengths of colored ribbon, cord, or embroidery floss
- scented blessing oil
- food and drink to share

To Work This Spell

Chant the invocation to Baldur either taking turns or together.

Here is one possible invocation to Baldur:

Bright Baldur, son of Odin,
you who were beloved by all.
Lend your amiable ways to our rite
so that we may be fast friends and true to each other.
May these ties we have forged be a joy
and something we can celebrate down the
years as we age and grow together.
Let us treasure this friendship we have forged.
Our friendship can be something
that is more than just the two of us together—
it can be something greater and better.
Be with us, Baldur, and help us to be fast friends!

Here is an alternative invocation to Balder to attract a new friend:

Bright Balder, son of Odin,
you who were a friend to all.
Help me to gain a new friend—
someone who will be a companion
and share my life as I share their life.
Let us become fast friends
and boon companions.

Sit down with your friend and each color half of the page together. Ideally, each person should do one blossom, one ring, one column, etc. Have fun! Laugh, talk, or sing while you do this. Do not worry about whose half looks better or who works faster. Enjoy the fact that you each bring something unique to the finished art.

Discuss your affirmation together before it is written in at the bottom. Be sure you agree upon what it should say.

When the page is done, tie your strands of hair, ribbon, floss, or yarn together at the top. While chanting your affirmation together, take turns weaving a braid. It can be as long or as short as you desire. When it is finished, tie another knot at the bottom or secure it with a tightly tied piece of ribbon, floss, etc. The two of you will remain connected on a soul level so long as the cord remains woven.

Consecrate the finished cord with some scented oil to seal in the spell.

Give each other a hug and share some food.

Close your circle and relax.

Display the finished art and cord somewhere where each person can enjoy it, or make a color copy for each friend to take home.

Note: If the friendship ever comes to an end, both parties should come together to do a formal parting. This is easily done by unbraiding the cord and then burning it along with the colored Friendship page. Let's hope that this won't have to happen!

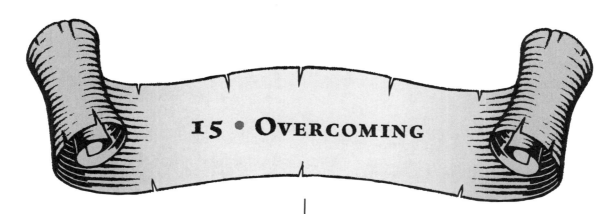

15 • OVERCOMING

OVERCOMING: being able to work hard and triumph over adversity, addiction, obsession, and other unpleasant ways of life. Working this hard to attain a goal may require some sort of sacrifice.

Everyone has bad habits and ways of life that may not be wholesome and healthy. Sometimes these faults become overwhelming and take over a life to the detriment of everything else. This is addiction. Addiction is difficult but can be overcome with hard work and steady application to reach the goal. Just like climbing a mountain, it isn't done all at once. It is done in stages. Sometimes you have to go back to move forward, but eventually you can reach the top, the pinnacle, your goal of overcoming whatever it is you need to.

Sometimes the task is to dedicate yourself to something, sacrifice to do what you need, and then apply yourself to the task and eventually get what you want. The ordeal may be difficult, but the gain is well worth the pain and sacrifice.

The Symbols

We chose symbols that have been used for overcoming throughout various cultures. If you have others, feel free to draw or paste them in for yourself.

A climber stands triumphant on top of a mountain. A summit flag of achievement is held proudly aloft before being planted atop the mountain. The mountain has clouds around the middle, but the summit is clear. Sometimes you cannot see much while you are on the way up, but once you are on top, you can clearly see where you have been and what it took to get there.

A sun that is bright and unobstructed shows achievement. The sun's rays encircle the triumphant climber.

Chains that are broken in the middle symbolize the difficulties overcome.

Look for the astrological symbol for Saturn (the planet of barriers and boundaries but also hard work and goals achieved after long and hard work) and the astrological symbol for the sign of Virgo, the sign of the Virgin/Goddess. Virgos are diligent, detail oriented, hard working, and willing to do whatever it takes to get what they want.

Find the rune Sowilo, which means victory.

We also used the thumbs-up sign, meaning success, well done, and victory.

Ritual for Overcoming

Suggested Colors
Purple is the color of spirit and the mysteries.

Red, orange, and yellow are the colors of fire, the sun, and the energy of re-creation.

Brown is the color of the earth and this material world we live in.

Green is the color of growth and spring.

Blue is the color of calm and dedication.

Black is the color of hitting bottom and dealing with harsh realities.

Silver and gold symbolize the worth of what we gain from working hard.

Special Supplies

- a black candle for the bad being overcome
- a white candle for the heights you can attain through overcoming

To Work This Spell

Recall the events that have brought you to this ritual. Think about what needs changing in your life and what you want to achieve. Know that seeing what you want is the first step to achieving it.

Light the black candle for the old habits you are leaving behind or the state of being ignorant.

We have chosen Odin as the deity for the overcoming ritual. Odin the All-Father went through an ordeal to attain the runes, the knowledge of what they mean, and the wisdom to use them appropriately. The Havamal details his ordeal: for nine nights he hung alone on the tree, none gave him food or drink, he dedicated himself to himself, and after his sacrifice he was given the runes and the knowledge to use them.

Odin the All-Father who traded his eye for knowledge.
Help me to overcome,
Help me to learn and grow,
Help me to become a better person
through my hard work and sacrifice.
I sacrifice up my old self
that I may learn and grow,
that I may overcome,
that I may triumph and succeed.
Help me to become a new person, renewed and whole,
able to live a confident and healthy life.

Take time to color your picture spell.

Once the picture is finished, visualize yourself as the new person you want to become. Know you can attain this goal.

Light the white candle for the new you.

Extinguish the black candle, symbolizing your sacrifice fulfilled.

Say something like:

All-Father Odin, help me to achieve my goal.
Grant me your determination and dedication.
Show me the way that I may triumph
and make a new life for myself.
Help me persevere in my goal.

Thank whatever deities or elements you have called upon for attending on your behalf.

Close your circle and relax, confident that you are making a good start for attaining your ultimate goal.

Display your art somewhere appropriate as a reminder of the goal you have set for yourself, the work you need to do, and the work that you have already done. Realize it may take time for you to attain your goal, but know you have it within yourself to get what you want and to get where you need to be. Stick with it. Victory is within your grasp!

OVERCOMING

16 · CUT-AWAY

CUT-AWAY: sometimes you need to cut yourself away from your past, old habits, bad influences, or people you no longer want or need in your life, etc.

Cutting things out of your life can be painful, but ultimately it is cleansing and allows you to start anew with a clean slate. Cutting away is not undertaken lightly and should be contemplated deeply before actually making the effort.

By cutting away things no longer needed, wanted, or relevant to your life, you can free yourself from influences that are tying you down, holding you back, and preventing you from being the whole person you want to be. It's a difficult thing to do, but you feel much lighter and freer after it is accomplished.

This ritual is best done while the moon is waning between full and new.

A cut-away can be done to eliminate people from your life who are difficult, demanding, and destructive to you. This would be an ex or someone you feel is pulling energy from you while you get no beneficial return. This is something of a last resort after you have tried all measures to create safe and healthy boundaries.

This ritual uses a harsh goddess, Mother Kali, who may seem fearsome to some. To get best results, you should be serious in your intention, give her an appropriate offering (like a cup of clear cool water, a piece of fruit, or a beautiful flower), be respectful and grateful for her help, and be sure to properly close the circle down when finished. Be sure you really want what you ask for. When you pray to Mother Kali, it's like a child crying out to a mother—and Mother Kali always responds like a mother who hears her child crying.

The Symbols

We chose symbols that have been used for cutting away throughout various cultures. If you have others, feel free to draw or paste them in for yourself.

A sickle cutting a rope symbolizes the severing of ties, the releasing of bonds, and the ending of a difficult situation.

The full moon is a point of culmination, and now the moon will wane, losing light each night until it is invisible. The time of the waning moon is a time for endings, decrease, and things that you want to go away.

We chose lightning and fire as symbols of things that change and end. The lightning can blast apart bad things, unwanted ties, and outdated traditional ways. Fire, as it burns, consumes material things, cleanses, and removes disease, rot, and unhealthy influences.

Look for the astrological glyphs for the planet Mars (the god of war and violence, and also ego and getting your own way) and the planet Pluto (planet of urban renewal, destruction before rebuilding—the force that clears and cleanses, like an atomic bomb).

Find the rune Hagalaz, depicting destruction that clears the way for renewal and transformation.

A set of footprints shows the power to walk away from what you want to be rid of.

A Cut-Away Ritual

Suggested Colors

Red is a color for Mars, energy, and blood.

Black is a color of ending and mourning.

Brown is a color of grounding energies and sending unwanted energies into the earth.

Yellow and orange are colors of cleansing fire.

Indigo is the color of insight and perception.

White and silver are the colors of the waning moon, purity, and cleansing.

Special Supplies

- descriptions of something or someone you want to eliminate from your life

- a pen or pencil

- clean paper

- an ashtray or some other fireproof vessel in which to burn paper or rope safely

- a red candle, a black candle, and a white candle

To Work This Spell

Light the red and black candles and invite Kali, the goddess of endings, to aid you in your cut-away rite. Here is a Mother Kali invocation:

Great Mother Kali, she who destroys so
that the new may take root:
help me eliminate from my life that which is unwanted.
Give me the courage and will to cut away
that which does not help me.
Let me be free of the influence that is harming me,
holding me back, draining my energy,
squandering my resources.
Give me the will and power to cut
away so that I may be free.

Color and decorate the Cut-Away page.

Write the name of the person or habit you are cutting away on the paper. Put your energy into that paper as you think about that person or habit and how they are making your life difficult.

Tear the paper with the name of the person you want to eliminate from your life into small pieces, visualizing the ties to them dissolving and being unable to be reformed.

Place the remnants of your spell in the fireproof container. Light them on fire, and make sure they are burnt totally—you may need several matches or lightings to get it all done. Make sure that you are in a space where fire will not cause a problem and that there is something to extinguish the fire should it get out of hand. Be safe.

Once you have ashes, stir them, making sure the fire is totally out. Know you have accomplished your purpose.

Extinguish the red and black candles.

Light the white candle.

Thank Mother Kali and whatever other deities or elements you have called upon for attending on your behalf.

Great Mother Kali,
thank you for your help in my cut-away rite.
Thank you for helping me make a new life—
a new life with healthy ties,
a new life with new opportunities,
a new life where I am free to live as I like.
Thank you, Mother Kali, for my freedom!

Close your circle and put out the white candle. Know you are free of those old influences. Place the ashes in the toilet and flush them away. You are flushing away the bad influences.

Display your art somewhere you can see and appreciate it. Know you are free from those old, unwanted influences. Once a full moon cycle has passed, remove the art and burn it or otherwise destroy it and throw it away. This art should never be retained, as you are then retaining the bad influences.

CUT-AWAY

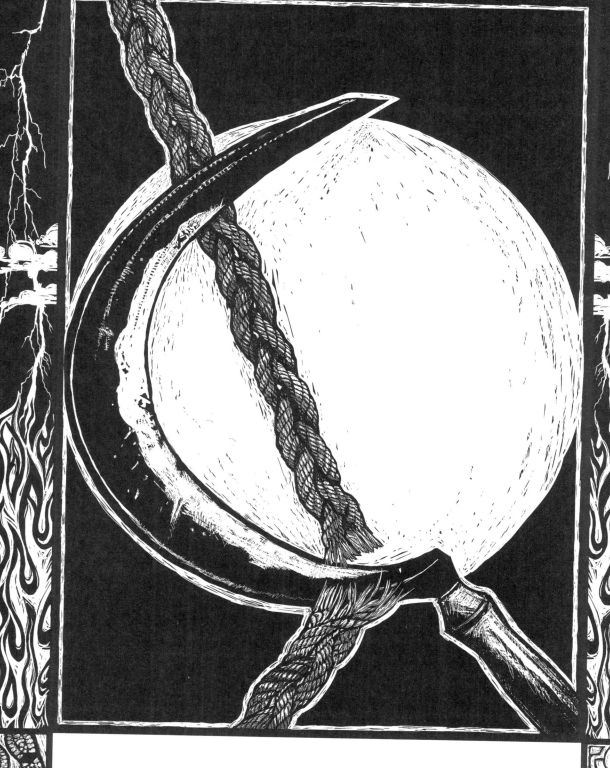

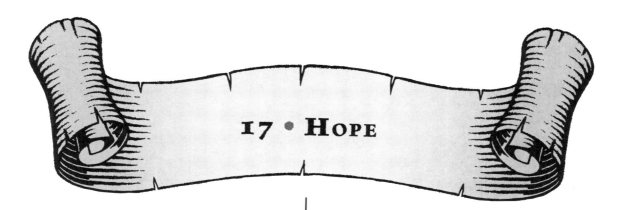

HOPE: the emotion that allows us to get through difficult times.

The hope that things will get better—that we can gain our dreams, that we can make things as good as we can. Hope was the last thing to come out of Pandora's box after all the ills and evils were released, so that we can endure them and persevere.

With hope we can endure most any ill, and using the positive energy of hope we can make things better for ourselves. Positive energy can make miracles happen, and hope brings positive energy to any situation.

The Symbols

We chose symbols that have been used for hope throughout various cultures. If you have others, feel free to draw or paste them in for yourself.

A pregnant woman symbolizes the hope of a new person and their potentialities and possibilities. The spiral on her belly shows the Goddess is alive in all creation, and the eight-pointed star at the center is the seed of potential that can grow to almost anything we can imagine.

Wings show that hope can fly anywhere—it can carry you out of a bad place and carry you into good places where you are safe and can grow and prosper.

We used stars of many shapes and sizes. The five-pointed star of action and humanity, the six-pointed star of balance and Kabbalistic energies, the seven-pointed star of the planets and the realms beyond our own, the eight-pointed star of deity and manifestation.

Look for an anchor, the mariner's symbol of hope for a safe harbor, and a butterfly, symbol of spirituality and hope.

Ritual for Hope

Suggested Colors

Yellow is a good color for confidence, vibrant energy, and a sunny disposition.

Green is a color of new growth, hope, and healing.

Purple and violet are colors of psychic energies, acceptance, and mysticism.

Brown is a color of manifestation on the material plane.

Indigo is the color of insight and perception.

Red is the color of courage and action.

White is a color of honesty, balance, and purity.

Special Supplies

- a symbol of whatever situation you need to have hope for

- blooming flowers (real or representations) to show that hope has blossomed and manifested in your life

- a white candle

To Work This Spell

Light the candle and invite the goddess Isis to help you have hope, no matter how desperate the situation.

A favorite Isis invocation is:

> O mighty Isis, sister-wife of slain Osiris,
> you never gave up hope that
> you could resurrect your beloved.
> You searched and when you needed,
> you constructed your hope.
> Isis, grant me perseverance.
> Isis, grant me patience.
> Isis, grant me wisdom to know
> when to accept what the universe brings and
> when to go out and create my own hope.
> Isis, help me to hope with confidence
> and the surety that I will prevail.

Color and decorate the Hope page.

Write your personal affirmation in the box at the bottom of the page. Say the affirmation out loud three times (or chant it, sing it, or shout it multiple times) to empower the spell.

When finished, thank Isis and whatever other deities or elements you have called upon for attending on your behalf.

> O mighty Isis, reunited with your beloved,
> let me gain the fruits of my hope.
> Help me to know when my hope has manifested.
> Grant me the serenity of hope manifest.

Close your circle and relax, confident that you have hope and can prevail.

Display your art somewhere you can see and appreciate it. Feel the hope it brings whenever you see it. Know where there is hope, the possibilities are endless.

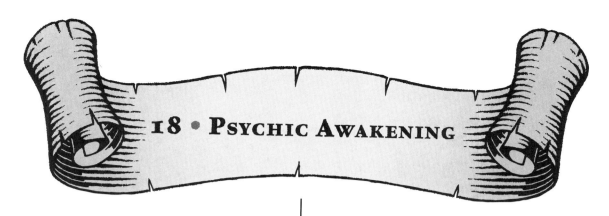

18 • PSYCHIC AWAKENING

PSYCHIC AWAKENING: the ability to see beyond the veils of the mundane world, and to see with the third eye whatever may be out there for you to see.

To awaken psychically is to gain the skill and judgment to use psychic gifts well and properly, and to help others and yourself with newfound knowledge and understanding. Even though something may seem frightening, it is not material and cannot harm us unless we allow it to.

Using psychic abilities is the essence of magick. Doing magick can help awaken your psychic abilities, but awakening your psychic abilities can help you do better magick—it's an endless circle of skill and ability that create results.

Start slow, but as you practice and become more skilled in using and controlling your abilities, you will find you can bring those psychic skills into your everyday life and allow yourself a wider viewpoint and bring about changes necessary to meet your goals and be more effective in your life.

Everybody has some sort of psychic skill and ability; the point is to maximize what you have and make the most of your abilities. Hone those psychic skills!

The Symbols

We chose symbols that have been used for psychic awakening throughout various cultures. If you have others, feel free to draw or paste them in for yourself.

The third eye—the ultimate symbol of psychic awareness—enables you to see without eyes and discern what is "out there." Once the psychic senses are awakened, it is like opening your third eye, allowing you to see what you could not see with your physical eyes. You need to practice using your metaphysical eye so you can see clearly and truly.

The moon with a face—the man in the moon—shows the understanding that the moon symbolizes the emotional, psychic, and more intuitive side of yourself. You can use your intuition and emotions to reach out beyond yourself and discern what cannot be obtained by "normal" means.

The Goddess—without specific form or face—shows all psychic talent is a gift of the Goddess, and you need to honor her to be able to take full use of those abilities. She will guide and help you as you learn to use your newfound skills. She will also show you how to use those skills with honor, ethics, and right action.

The sky with clouds and stars shows you can see beyond what is easily apparent and gain insights "beyond the stars." Looking outward, our psychic senses can perceive well beyond what any technology can show us.

The lotus rests on the water, but beneath the water is most of the plant and other things which may be hidden by the lotus's flowers and leaves. The expanding ripples on the water remind you that water is emotion, and emotion is the realm of the Goddess. By exercising your psychic gifts, you are in the realm of the Goddess.

Look for the astrological symbols of the Moon (the planet of psychic ability), Pisces (the sign of the psychic and mystic), Cancer (the sign of the intuitive and sensitive), and Neptune (the planet of illusion, mysticism, psychic awareness, and the ability to pierce the veils between the worlds).

Ritual for Psychic Awakening

Suggested Colors

Purple is a good color for psychic abilities, magick, and the mystical realm.

Blue is a color of emotion, calm, and depths of understanding.

Green is a color of growth and health.

White is the color of the moon's reflected light, purity, balance, and truth.

Gold is the color of riches and rewards, symbolizing our new psychic gifts.

Light blue is the color of the sky and delicate skills.

Special Supplies

- a reflective surface, such as a mirror, bowl of water, or crystal, to use as a surface through which to see with your third eye

- a cord or ribbon to symbolize the limits of your physical self, reminding you that you cannot be harmed by things that are not material

- a blue candle and a purple candle, placed on either side of the drawing as you work

To Work This Spell

Light the candles and invite the Goddess into your space to help and guide you in finding and using your psychic skills well and ethically. Here is a Goddess invocation for awakening psychic ability:

Goddess, Great Mother of us all,
grant me the ability to see with my third eye.
Allow me to open my psychic abilities so I may see clearly
and use my skills to help myself and others.
Grant me the judgment and discernment
to use my psychic skills
with ethics, right action, and deep understanding.
Help me to see clearly and with understanding.

Color and decorate the Psychic Awakening page. As you work, relax and allow your mind's eye (the third eye) to open and start looking around. Be calm and accepting of whatever you see, and thank the Goddess for whatever visions you receive.

Every so often, allow your gaze to rest on the reflective surface. Defocus your eyes and allow your mind to roam as it will, and accept whatever you see or do not see. Sometimes not getting anything can be as profound as seeing something.

Write your personal affirmation in the box at the bottom of the page. Say the affirmation out loud three times (or chant it, sing it, or shout it multiple times) to empower the spell.

Relax and close your eyes, breathe quietly and deeply, and clear your mind of mundane clutter and noise. Allow yourself to receive whatever the Goddess may choose to send to you. Spend at least ten minutes just quietly being open to the impressions and sights you may have.

When finished, write down whatever you have seen or discerned, then thank the Goddess and whatever other deities or elements you have called upon for attending on your behalf.

Close your circle and relax, confident that your psychic awakening has begun and will grow with use and right action.

Display your art somewhere you can see and appreciate it. Close your eyes and become aware of your newfound psychic awareness and what insights it may bring to your life. Use those insights to help yourself and others.

PSYCHIC AWAKENING

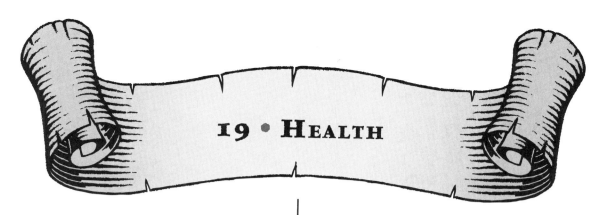

HEALTH: the state where your body and mind are operating at maximum ability.

A healthy body has no foreign organisms causing disease. When you can do whatever you need and want to with your body, without harm or restrictions from problems—be they from disease, injury, or a state of less-than-best conditions in your body—you have obtained health.

Health is also a process whereby you work to make your body the best it can be through proper diet, exercise, and right living, and the ability to maintain that good condition through time, ideally for the rest of your life. A healthy mindset is having the knowledge to do what you need to keep your body in top condition, the will to keep at it, and the satisfaction derived from having a healthy body and mind. As long as you have your health, the rest will follow.

Aesclepius was the Greek god of healing, and Hygiea, his daughter, was the goddess of health and cleanliness. Aesclepius was son of Apollo and Coronis, who was unfaithful to Apollo and was killed for it. On her funeral pyre the unborn Aesclepius was cut from her womb, and Apollo took him to Chiron, the king of the centaurs, to be raised and taught.

There were several temples and schools dedicated to Aesclepius throughout the ancient world. Aesclepius was killed by Hades because he brought people back to life, and Hades was angered as he thought no more shades would come to Tartarus because of these acts. After his death, Aesclepius was placed in the night sky by Zeus as Ophiucus, the serpent bearer.

The Symbols

We chose symbols that have been used for health and healing throughout various cultures. If you have others, feel free to draw or paste them in for yourself.

The figure represents you or someone who needs healing: a vibrant, healthy person radiating power, physical energy, self-confidence, self-acceptance, and self-love to the very roots of their flaming hair.

The chakra energy centers are open and unblocked. They form a rainbow spectrum of pure color that connects the figure's physical, mental, and spiritual planes. The heart is light (both in color and weight) with happiness and contentment.

The wings of a guardian angel (higher self) protectively surround and keep the figure safe from harm.

The arms are spread wide, palms out, in a gesture of openness and friendship. The stance is also open, giving a grounded center of balance. Behind the figure light emanates from this grounded, balanced center.

As the old proverb states, an apple a day keeps the doctor away.

The rod of Aesclepius is the legendary wand that symbolizes healing. This symbol is nearly universal, found in ancient Egypt, Mesopotamia, and India, where it is always a symbol of harmony and balance. In the Hermetic Tradition it is a symbol of spiritual awakening and has been likened to the kundalini serpents of Hindu mysticism.

Rays of energy and well-being show vitality and wholeness have chased away any feelings of sickness and negativity.

Ritual for Healing

Suggested Colors
The chakras are traditionally colored from bottom to top as red, orange, yellow, green, blue, indigo, and violet for the crown chakra. Their colors are pure and vibrant.

Green is a traditional color of healing.

Red is the color of blood, the vital fluid that carries oxygen and nutrients throughout the body.

Yellow and orange are colors of energy, vitality, and action.

White is a color of purity and cleanliness.

Special Supplies
- a cup containing a healthy, nourishing drink—something that's natural and pure, like water

- a picture of you or the person to be healed (If you are doing the spell for another person, make sure that they know you are doing it, and that you have their permission to do the spell for them. Doing a healing on an unknowing or unwilling person is unethical. Make sure the other person knows you are doing this and is willing to have you do it for them.)

- a green candle, a red candle, and a white candle

To Work This Spell
Light the green candle and invite Aesclepius and Hygeia to grant you health and vitality.

One possible invocation of Aesclepius and Hygeia is:

Divine physician, son of Apollo,
Aesclepius, grant me health!
Help me overcome _____
(whatever you need to fix)
and let me learn how to keep myself
in the best way that I can.
Divine Hygeia, daughter of Aesclepius,
Grant me health through a clean and
well-maintained body and mind.
Divine healers, show me the way, and I will
do my part to get and stay healthy.
Let me get healthy,
let me get strong and vital in body,
let me get healthy in my mind and emotions.
Grant me health!

Light the red candle and ask Aesclepius and Hygeia for the will and determination to keep at your task so you can be successful in the end.

Color and decorate the Health page. As you color the chakras, feel the energy moving up through your body (or the body of the person you are doing the working for), filling you (or them) with vitality and energy.

Look at the picture and visualize healing energy flowing through you (or the person you are doing the working for).

As you color the picture, visualize yourself (or the person you are doing the spell for) as the disease/problem/condition leaves the body, being washed away with healing energy and the body's correct functioning. Know it may take a while, but that in the end the body will be whole, functioning properly, and well in every way.

Write your personal affirmation in the box at the bottom of the page. Say the affirmation out loud four times (or chant it, sing it, or shout it) to empower the spell.

Light the white candle and repeat the Aesclepius and Hygeia invocation.

Take the cup and drink the liquid. Feel it flowing into your body and know its healing properties are being carried into every cell, and washing away all impurities, disease and unwanted conditions. Know you can and will be healed, and you can maintain good health with right action on your part. (If doing the spell for another, send the healing energies to them.)

When finished, thank Aesclepius, Hygeia, and whatever other deities or elements you have called upon for attending on your behalf.

Close your circle and relax, feeling the healthy energies permeating your body. Know the healing has begun, and understand what you need to do to get and stay healthy for the rest of your life.

Display your art somewhere you can see and appreciate it. Every time you look at it, feel the healing energies working in your body and mind, and visualize your body healing itself and becoming whole and vital.

20 • PROTECTION

PROTECTION: being safe and secure in your living environment, having the resources to be secure, having the strength and ability to make yourself secure, and having people you can call on for help, should you need it, and knowing there are people out there whose job it is to keep everyone safe.

Heracles was a hero in ancient Greece whose worship spread all around the Mediterranean. He was known as the protector of mankind. He was strong and resourceful, and in his twelve labors he rid the ancient world of many monsters who menaced humanity. Many of the monsters were defeated by strength and warrior prowess alone, but a few were defeated by cunning and even trickery. Heracles did whatever he needed to do to make the world safer for all. His many sons were also heroes and wandered the ancient world righting wrongs, defeating monsters and tyrants, and making the world safe.

The Symbols

We chose symbols that have been used for protection throughout various cultures. If you have others, feel free to draw or paste them in for yourself.

An upright pentagram's five points—symbolizing spirit, air, fire, water, and earth—reach toward a higher spiritual plane.

The hammer Mjolnir is the favorite weapon of the Norse god Thor. As a god of thunder who symbolized strength and fertilizing rain, Thor was a hero to the everyday peasant farmers, who worshiped him as a protector of family, flocks, and crops.

A spider's web is one of Mother Nature's barriers to protect us from nasty flying pests.

A keyhole is the entry point to a lock protecting valuables from anyone who does not have the right key.

The Hand of God and wings of a holy guardian angel are powerful protective symbols.

The Horned One is protector of the herd. The reversed pentagram upon his brow brings spirit down into earthly matter.

Hedgerows were used in old Europe to mark the edges of property or villages. Hedges separated the safe "known" world from the unsafe "unknown" beyond.

Look for more protective symbols: a shield, a turtle, the Eye of Horus, and the rune Thurisaz (meaning thorn, defense, or Thor's hammer).

Ritual of Protection

Suggested Colors
Red is a color of strength and power.

Green and blue are colors of safety.

Silver and gold are colors symbolizing wealth and possessions.

Brown is a color of solidity and security.

Special Supplies

- 2 keys (They should be old keys that aren't used anymore, maybe for a house or car you no longer own or occupy, or maybe old-fashioned skeleton keys. Even blank keys will work. Do not use your present door or car key. These keys will not be used for anything except a magickal purpose.

- 2 brown candles

To Work This Spell

Light the brown candles and invite Heracles to join you in your spell.

One possible invocation of Heracles is:

Lion-clad, divine Heracles, protector of mankind,
Help me to protect myself, my space, and those I love.
Grant me the skill, strength, knowledge, and cunning
to make myself and my space safe.
Show me the resources to protect myself appropriately.
Help me to make myself and my space
invisible to those who would harm me,
try to invade my space,
or take what is rightfully mine.
Divine Heracles, protect me!

Color and decorate the Protection page. You can incorporate your keys into the design, perhaps by gluing them to the page or just allow them to rest beside you as you work, absorbing the energies of your spell as you work it. Or you can glue one to the page and leave one beside you.

Look at the picture and think about your living environment. Look at it with the eyes of a thief or invader; try to see the places you need to reinforce and make

more secure. Maybe you can devise places to hide valuables, if you want to do so, or maybe make a plan for adding security to your living space.

As you color the picture, visualize a hedge of thorns surrounding your space, high and impenetrable to anyone who is not welcomed by you. Visualize a force shield around yourself, making you safe as you move around in the world.

Write your personal affirmation in the box at the bottom of the page. Say the affirmation out loud twelve times (or chant it, sing it, or shout it) to empower the spell.

For protection of living space: take your key and glue it into the picture or put it on a string and hang it at the main door of your living space. Know this key symbolizes the protection you have built into your living space. It holds the energy of your spell.

For protection of your person: take your key and glue it into the picture or put it on a string and wear it under your clothes. Know this key symbolizes the protection surrounding you. It holds the energy of your spell.

When finished, thank Heracles and whatever other deities or elements you have called upon for attending on your behalf.

Close your circle and relax, feeling the energies surrounding your living space and yourself. Know these energies are shielding you, making you safe and protected from those who would harm or violate you or your living space.

Display your art somewhere you can see and appreciate it. Every time you look at it, visualize the shields you constructed and add energy to them, making them stronger and more effective. Feel how your keys are tied into the spell and how they carry the energies of your spell to keep you and your living space safe.

PROTECTION

21 • BETTER WORLD

BETTER WORLD: a place that is better than before, making things better, realizing dreams for a better world, living on a planet that is healthy and sustainably managed, making positive change for the benefit of all.

A better world is something we all would like to have, but what that may be is not necessarily the same for everyone, and it is not something that is accomplished in one act. Rather, it will take people from all over the planet, each making their own contribution and working together in harmony, to coordinate their efforts and harmonize their wishes and dreams.

Creating a better world does not happen quickly, but each person can, through their own efforts coordinated with others', change the world incrementally. Many people, all working on their own projects, can effect real change, and as they gain momentum, they make the positive changes real, permanent, and beneficial for all. Everyone can do their part, large or small, as they are able, and bit by bit things are accomplished. Once started, the positive changes come more and faster with each person who adds their energy and will to the project. It is a never-ending cycle, but each step adds momentum to the larger intent. It can and will be accomplished as people pledge to do their bit as they can.

The Symbols
We chose symbols that show unity and sustainability and suggest people can work together to make the world a better place. If you have others, feel free to add them.

The globe with a peace symbol overlaying it shows that peace can be accomplished if we all work toward it together. Peace brings prosperity, and using that prosperity we can make positive change that can affect everyone. The globe is ringed with people hand in hand, showing we can all work together if we choose to do so. By working together, we can accomplish more than we can as individuals.

Look for the rainbow, a symbol of hope, peace, and unity in diversity. The many colors of the rainbow symbolize that it will take all peoples working together to achieve a better world. There are many paths to achieve those aims; there is no one single solution but many solutions that will apply in various places as appropriate. The doves of peace, carrying olive branches, also show peace is an attainable goal. The olive branches symbolize peace and plenty because the olive is a thoroughly useful plant, providing shade, useful wood for building and warmth, and food as well as oil.

Find a series of X's, which are the rune Gifu, symbolizing gifts, plenty, and bounty, sharing gifts for the common good and success.

Bay laurel, a symbol of cooperation and success, was woven into laurel crowns worn by winners and those who have made concrete accomplishments that make the world a better place.

The astrological symbols for the fixed signs of Taurus, Leo, Scorpio, and Aquarius show that lasting change can be made manifest, making concrete progress, and a fixity of purpose toward accomplishing material and useful goals. Fixed signs make lasting changes.

Ritual for a Better World

Suggested Colors

Green is a color of abundance, health, and healing.

Pink is a color of peace and beneficial works.

Brown is a color of the earth and wood, symbols of material things.

Blue is the color of a clear, calm mind that is open to new possibilities.

Red and orange are colors of will and energy for making things manifest.

A rainbow has all colors, showing all the possibilities that can be made manifest with people of good will working together.

Special Supplies

- a pink candle for peace
- a red or orange candle for will and energy
- a green candle for healing and growth
- pictures or symbols of what you think a better world means

To Work This Spell

Clear your mind and relax. Allow yourself to become open to what the universe has to offer you. Realize you need to keep an open mind so you can take advantage of the opportunities that present themselves to you.

Light your pink, red/orange, and green candles for the triple intents that can bring about a better world.

Call on the goddess Gaea to help you know what you need to do to help create a better world for yourself and the rest of humanity.

Say something like:

Earth Mother Gaea, mother of us all,
embodiment of our living planet, giver of gifts,
grant me the will and skills to help make
a better world for myself and others.
Guide my efforts,
help me understand what needs to be done
and the means to make it happen.
Let me take advantage of whatever
opportunities are presented to me,
help me to act in appropriate ways,
help me to find kindred souls to work together,
let me be an agent for positive change.

Take time to color your picture spell.

Write your personal affirmation at the bottom. Chant it out loud and hear your intent fly out to the universe.

When you have finished, thank the goddess Gaea:

Earth Mother Gaea, mother of us all,
embodiment of our living planet, giver of gifts,
thank you for your guidance and knowledge.
Thank you for helping me find my will and determination.
Thank you for whatever people have helped me in my efforts.
Thank you for whatever positive change I may accomplish.
May your love and insight guide me in my life
so I can keep working toward positive change
and help make the world a better place for all.

Thank whatever deities or elements you have called upon for attending on your behalf.

Close your circle and relax, knowing you are an agent for positive change. You can help make the world a better place for all.

Display your art somewhere appropriate as a reminder of the better world that you are helping to create.

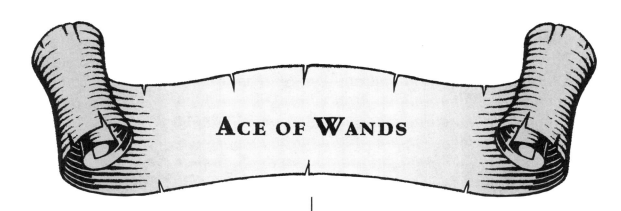

ACE OF WANDS

ACE OF WANDS: the pure expression of the element of fire.

Fire is the element of energy, inspiration, and zeal. A fire can warm or, when out of control, destroy. Mastering fire was the first step for mankind on the way to civilization. The fire of the soul can give the energy to create and pass along skills and ideas. Elusive in nature, fire is yet the servant of man, allowing us to transmute things for our use. How you choose to use your inner fire will determine how you create and inspire and are inspired.

The Symbols
We chose symbols that have been used for the element of fire throughout various cultures. If you have others, feel free to draw or paste them in for yourself.

- A caduceus is a winged wand surrounded by twin serpents. Sometimes it is called the staff of Hermes. The serpents represent the kundalini force, the vital force within every person that starts from the base chakra and twines around the spine to emerge at the top of the head. It symbolizes the power within each of us to create and be vital. An acorn is at the bottom of the caduceus and the two flaming torches, showing how a great thing can grow from a small seed. The top of the caduceus is a pinecone, turning the wand to a thyrsus, a symbol of male vitality and also Dionysus, the great god of passion and ecstasy.

- A sun shines behind the wand, being the most fiery of all the astrological planets and the center of our solar system.

- Two lions on a mountain emerging from a grassy plain show the power of fire and symbolize the astrological sign of Leo.

- Sticks as wands adorn the sides, symbolizing fire.

- Look for the astrological symbols for Aries (the sign of cardinal fire), Leo (the sign of fixed fire), and Sagittarius (the sign of mutable fire). The fire signs are the inspirational signs of the zodiac.

- Find the astrological symbol for the sun, the most fiery of the astrological planets and the center of our solar system. Without the sun's spark of life, we would not be active beings.

Ace of Wands Ritual

Suggested Colors
Yellow and orange are the colors of the sun, action, and mentality.

Red and orange are colors of fire and energy.

Brown is a color of wood and material things.

Green is a color of growing things, life, and health.

Gold is a color of wealth and the sun.

Blue is a color of the sky and calm emotion.

Special Supplies
- a white candle to manifest fire

- a red candle and a yellow candle for the colors of fire and the sun

To Work This Spell

Light the white candle. Watch the flame grow. Hold your hand near the flame to feel the heat. Feel the energy in your body, waiting to be used.

Light the red and yellow candles.

Say something like:

> *Ace of Wands, symbol of Fire Guardians*
> *of the Watchtowers of the South,*
> *creatures of fire, I welcome you to my circle.*
> *Teach me of your essence and energies*
> *that I may use them in my life.*
> *Help me to integrate your energies*
> *to make me more complete.*

Take time to color your picture spell.

Write your personal affirmation at the bottom, and chant it out loud.

Once your picture is finished, place your hand near the flame of the white candle. Feel the warmth of the fire, and the energy of your body that was used to color and empower your picture. Know your energy is in the picture, ready to go out into the universe.

Say something like:

> *Guardians of the Watchtowers of the South, creatures of fire,*
> *may there be peace between us now and always.*
> *Thank you for your presence in my circle.*
> *Thank you for the lessons you have taught me.*
> *As you return to your eternal realms,*
> *I bid you a loving hail and farewell.*

Thank whatever deities or elements you have called upon for attending on your behalf.

Close your circle and relax, confident that you have integrated the energies of fire into your being.

Display your art somewhere appropriate as a reminder of what fire means to you and what lessons you have learned from fire.

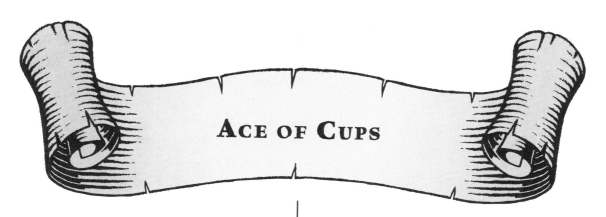

ACE OF CUPS

ACE OF CUPS: the pure expression of the element of water.

Water is the element of emotion, memory, feelings, intuition, the past, and remembrance. Water exists in many forms. As liquid, it flows and can erode and shape anything on earth through its relentless action. As ice, it can scrape and grind and break apart the strongest rock. As water vapor, it condenses to make clouds and eventually rain, which nourishes the earth. As steam, it can cleanse and scald and make energy for machines to run.

The Symbols

We chose symbols that have been used for the element of water throughout various cultures. If you have others, feel free to draw or paste them in for yourself.

- A cup rises from the water; water flows from the cup in streams and drops. It runneth over, showing more blessings and bounty than the cup can hold, and so they are spread around to any nearby.

- A circle is seen rising from the cup—is it the moon or something else?

- A circular design is behind the cup. The circle is a symbol of wholeness, of the circle of birth, life, death, and rebirth. The scallops at the edges of the circle are from Pennsylvania Dutch Hex symbolism, denoting ocean waves and smooth sailing through life.

- The cup rests on a lotus, a watery symbol associated with purity, rebirth, and divinity.

- Rays rising from the cup show this is a special vessel of energy as well as water.

- Fish swimming in water symbolize the life that water contains and sustains.

- Look for the astrological symbol for Pisces, the sign of mutable water. Possibly the most watery of the water signs, Pisces rules the oceans.

- Find the astrological symbol for Cancer, the sign of cardinal water; Cancer rules lakes and rivers.

- See the astrological symbol for Scorpio, the sign of fixed water; Scorpio rules all underground water, whether flowing or still.

- Find the glyph of Neptune—the planet of water flowing, deep mysteries, dreams, and visions.

Ace of Cups Ritual

Suggested Colors

Purple is the color of spirit and the mysteries.

Blue and green are colors of water and the seas.

Orange, white, and black are colors of goldfish swimming in a pool.

Rose is the color of dawn.

Silver is the color of the moon as she shines down upon the earth.

Gold is the color of wealth and mentality.

Special Supplies
- a blue candle and a green candle for the color of the seas
- a silver candle for the moon
- a small bowl of clear water

To Work This Spell

Hold the bowl of water in your hand. Feel the energy of the water. Dip your fingers into the water and anoint yourself with it to feel its essence on your skin.

Light the three candles.

Say something like:

> *Ace of Cups, vessel of water,*
> *Guardians of the Watchtowers of the West,*
> *creatures of water, I welcome you to my circle.*
> *Teach me of your essence and energies so*
> *that I may use them in my life.*
> *Help me to integrate your energies*
> *and make me more complete.*

Take time to color your picture spell.

Write your personal affirmation at the bottom and chant it out loud.

Once your picture is finished, take the bowl of water in your hand and drink the water. Feel the cool and refreshing water flow down your throat. Feel the energies of the water enter your being.

Say something like:

> *Guardians of the Watchtowers of the West,*
> *creatures of water,*
> *may there be peace between us now and always.*
> *Thank you for your presence in my circle.*
> *Thank you for the lessons you have taught me.*
> *As you return to your eternal realms,*
> *I bid you a loving hail and farewell.*

Thank whatever deities or elements you have called upon for attending on your behalf.

Close your circle and relax, confident that you have integrated the energies of water into your being.

Display your art somewhere appropriate as a reminder of what water means to you and what lessons you have learned from water.

ACE OF SWORDS

ACE OF SWORDS: the pure expression of the element of air.

Air is the element of mind, mentality, and thought. It can be a cooling breeze or a raging storm. If you don't have enough air, you can asphyxiate. Too much air can leave you breathless. It is the only invisible element, only perceived by its effects—the feeling of a breeze against your skin, seeing the trees as they bend in the wind. Air is everywhere, and we need our mind and our perceptions to be a conscious, thinking being. How you use your consciousness is your choice. How aware you are to all that is around you determines how you operate in life: aware and awake or on autopilot, not thinking about the here and now.

The Symbols
We chose symbols that have been used for the element of air throughout various cultures. If you have others, feel free to draw or paste them in for yourself.

- A sword is in the clouds, silhouetted by the crescent moon. Is it waxing or waning?

- A dragonfly rests along the hilt of the sword, an insect that is truly hermaphroditic, echoing the planet Mercury in its ability to take on the nature of the signs it resides in. Moon disks sit between the wings—one waxing, one waning—so there are three moons in the image.

- See Odin's ravens Hugin and Munin, thought and memory.

- Feathers adorn the sides, symbolizing birds and also how a feather can show the effects of air.

- Look for the astrological symbols for Gemini (the sign of mutable air), Libra (the sign of cardinal air), and Aquarius (the sign of fixed air). The air signs are the rational signs of the zodiac.

- Find the astrological symbol for Mercury, the messenger of the zodiac and most mental of the planets.

Ritual for Ace of Swords

Suggested Colors
Yellow is a color of mind and mental activity.

Blue is a color of the skies and of cool, rational thought.

White, gray, and black are the color of clouds, depending on what weather they bring.

Green, gold, blue, purple, and turquoise are colors that dragonflies manifest, iridescent and shimmering.

Silver is the color of the moon as she shines down upon the earth.

Pink is a color of peace and calm.

Special Supplies
- a white candle and a yellow candle for clear, untroubled thought

- a feather or piece of fluff

- a stick of incense and holder in whatever scent you feel is appropriate

To Work This Spell

Light the incense and watch the smoke rise, making the air visible. If it burns out, you can light another stick or just let it go.

Hold the feather or fluff in your hand, wave it around, and see how it catches the air.

Breathe deeply, allowing the air to fill your lungs. Feel it going in and out, refreshing your body and oxygenating your blood.

Light the two candles.

Say something like:

> *Ace of Swords, symbol of air,*
> *Guardians of the Watchtowers of the East,*
> *Creatures of air, I welcome you to my circle.*
> *Teach me of your essence and energies*
> *so that I may use them in my life.*
> *Help me to integrate your energies*
> *and make me more complete.*

Take time to color your picture spell.

Write your personal affirmation at the bottom and chant it out loud.

Once your picture is finished, take the feather or fluff in your hand. Wave it around again and watch how it moves through the air. Breathe deeply, allowing the air to fill your lungs. Feel it going in and out, refreshing your body and oxygenating your blood.

Say something like:

> *Guardians of the Watchtowers of the East,*
> *creatures of air,*
> *may there be peace between us now and always.*
> *Thank you for your presence in my circle.*
> *Thank you for the lessons you have taught me.*
> *As you return to your eternal realms,*
> *I bid you a loving hail and farewell.*

Thank whatever deities or elements you have called upon for attending on your behalf.

Close your circle and relax, confident that you have integrated the energies of air into your being.

Display your art somewhere appropriate as a reminder of what air means to you and what lessons you have learned from air.

ACE OF SWORDS

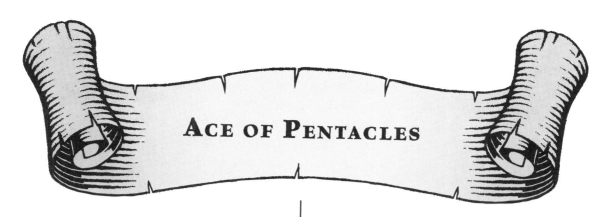

ACE OF PENTACLES

ACE OF PENTACLES: the pure expression of the element of earth.

Earth is the element of fertility, solid matter, prosperity, and material wealth. Earth manifests as fertile soil, barren sands, craggy hills, and impassible mountains. What aspect of earth you deal with and how it can manifest in your life is up to you. If you have fertile soil but plant nothing, then how can you expect a bountiful harvest? Barren rocks may seem forbidding, but they may also contain precious gemstones, which can be extracted with skilled work.

The Symbols
We chose symbols that have been used for the element of earth throughout various cultures. If you have others, feel free to draw or paste them in for yourself.

A pentacle stands in the earth. It is entwined with leaves from plants growing in the fertile soil.

An eight-spoked wheel symbolizes the flow of the seasons, the eight sabbats, the quarters and cross-quarters of the sun.

The fertile earth with growing plants. The roots of the plants entwine around rocks, which are also part of the earth.

Hills rising to mountains show earth reaching to the sky.

Sheaves of wheat symbolize the fertility and abundance that the earth, well managed, can provide.

Look for the astrological symbol for Taurus, the sign of fixed earth. Possibly the most earthy of the earth signs, Taurus rules the fertile soil and fields.

Find the astrological symbol for Virgo, the sign of mutable earth; Virgo rules forests and scrubland.

See the astrological symbol for Capricorn, the sign of cardinal earth. Capricorn rules mountains, craggy areas and deserts.

Find the glyph for Earth, the planet where we all live and the ultimate expression of the earth element.

Ace of Pentacles Ritual

Suggested Colors
Green is a color of life and growing things.

Yellow-gold is a color of ripened grain.

Brown and black are the colors of fertile soil.

Gray is a color of rock.

Green, silver, gold, and copper are colors of money and wealth.

Special Supplies
- a green candle for the color of growing things
- a gold candle for the color of ripened grain and wealth
- a brown candle for the fertility of the earth
- a small container of salt

To Work This Spell

Hold the container of salt in your hand. Feel the energy of the salt. Dip your fingers into the salt and rub it between your fingers.

Light the three candles.

Say something like:

> *Ace of Pentacles, symbol of earth,*
> *Guardians of the Watchtowers of the North,*
> *Creatures of earth,*
> *I welcome you to my circle.*
> *Teach me of your essence and energies*
> *so that I may use them in my life.*
> *Help me to integrate your energies*
> *and make me more complete.*

Take time to color your picture spell.

Write your personal affirmation at the bottom and chant it out loud.

Once your picture is finished, take the container of salt in your hand and place a few grains on your tongue. Taste the salt and draw its essence into yourself. Feel the energies of the earth enter your being.

Say something like:

> *Guardians of the Watchtowers of the North,*
> *creatures of earth,*
> *May there be peace between us now and always.*
> *Thank you for your presence in my circle.*
> *Thank you for the lessons you have taught me.*
> *As you return to your eternal realms,*
> *I bid you a loving hail and farewell.*

Thank whatever deities or elements you have called upon for attending on your behalf.

Close your circle and relax, confident that you have integrated the energies of earth into your being.

Display your art somewhere appropriate as a reminder of what earth means to you and what lessons you have learned from earth.

ACE of PENTACLES

COLOR MAGICK

Here is a list of colors and some of the common ideas about the meanings of each. Some of the meanings are contradictory, and some are attributed to more than one color. Use the colors that you like and that resonate with the purposes of your particular spell. If a certain color has a special meaning for you, then go with that.

White-Silver: All colors of the spectrum working together in harmony. Purity, cleanliness, light, day, chaos, Uranus, heat, energy, element of spirit, crown/seventh chakra. Also blankness, no color, absence of feeling or emotion, moon, lunar energy, winter, cold, ice, frost, death.

Pink: Love, romance, self-love, self-respect, friendship, caring, warmth, Venus, feminine energy, immature, can be irritating.

Red: Passion, energy, will, courage, war, blood, element of fire and energy, lust, sexuality, Mars, masculine energy, base or root/first chakra.

Orange: Creativity, heat, fire, mentality, Mercury, sacral/second chakra.

Yellow-Gold: Ego, confidence, mind, happiness, element of air and intellect, springtime, sunshine, sun, solar energy, creativity, leadership, wealth, harvest, solar/third chakra.

Yellow-Green: Disease, infection, sickness, decay, earthiness, spring, plant life, growth.

Green: Health and vitality, plant life and growth, prosperity, money, fertility, life, summer, peace, Venus, element of earth and stability, heart/fourth chakra.

Green-Blue: Oceans, sea-foam, water, calmness, tranquility, peace, melancholy, subdued emotions.

Blue: Emotions, calming, cooling, healing, cleanliness, element of water and emotion, clear skies, cold and frozen things, reason, rational thinking, communications, Jupiter, eloquence, throat/fifth chakra.

Indigo-Navy Blue: Intellect, communications, eloquence, deep space, deep water, deep thought, memory, psychic matters, Uranus, brow/sixth chakra, or third eye.

Purple-Violet: Spirituality, element of spirit, royalty, night, illusions, mist and fog, dreams, the collective unconscious, Neptune, the moon, lunar energy, crown/seventh chakra.

Brown: Earth, autumn, dirt, solid, practical, fertility, that which is discarded, boring, immovable, underground, muddied, unclear.

Gray: Fog, illusion, indeterminate, shades of gray, wishy-washy, slightly soiled, shadows, cool and damp, Neptune.

Black: Death, the underworld, earth, dirt, the void of space, the passing of time, the abyss, the veils between the worlds, psychopomps, ultimate peace, absence of energy, moistness, comfort, cold, boundaries, limits, harshness, the absence of color and light, dark, night, Saturn.

THE MAGICK OF THE RUNES

THE RUNES ARE letters of various alphabets used in Nordic/Germanic areas of Europe for writing, spellwork, and magick. The modern interpretations of the runes are just that—modern. There is little original material available as to how the runes were used in spellwork or magick. The runes have energies and correspondences that operate and can be used but never totally controlled. Once Christianity supplanted the original religions, the lore and magickal uses of the runes were lost. What we know now has been largely reconstructed, channeled, or surmised by authors from the Victorian era to the present. Even the name of each letter/symbol is an interpretation.

The Havamal Rune Poem states that Odin sacrificed himself to himself and after nine days of suffering, bound to a tree, he was shown the runes, their meanings, and how to use them.

The alphabet of the runes most commonly used today is the twenty-four character Elder Futhark. Sometimes people add a twenty-fifth "blank" rune, but that is a modern invention/addition.

There are many theories about the occult (or hidden) meanings of why the runes might be arranged in three Aetts (if there really is a mystical reason). One theory is that Freya's Aett deals with the creation of the universe. Hagall's Aett then takes the story through to Ragnarok, and Tyr's Aett picks up the story and details the emergence and existence of man.

Freya's Aett

1) Fehu (cattle, wealth): ᚠ

In ancient Germanic cultures, cattle were portable wealth. Prices of valuable things were measured in cattle. Cattle were domesticated, so the energies of this rune can be used with fair confidence it will operate as you expect it to. MEANINGS: Increase or preservation of personal wealth; increase of personal or environmental fertility; strengthening psychic powers; contact with the magickal powers or gods of the Vanir; wealth you create yourself; you can overcome obstacles if you continue on your current path; success; opportunity; growth.

2) Ur (aurochs, hoarfrost): ᚢ

The aurochs was a giant ox—their horns could be several feet long each. They were wild, massively powerful, and hunted to extinction by the modern age. They were an irresistible force, and the energy of this rune can get away from you because the aurochs could not be domesticated. Hoarfrost is a natural phenomenon that again cannot be controlled, though you can somewhat protect yourself from its effects. MEANINGS: Regaining or maintaining physical health by a massive infusion of energy; shaping unformed energy; self-understanding; single-mindedness toward a goal; unstoppable, berserker-like force; ancient, primal wisdom; berserk rage; strength and power; undergoing a rite of passage by mastering something within yourself; courage; determination; destiny.

3) Thurisaz (thorn, giant): ᚦ

Giants were a race that existed before men came to earth. They lived for today, with no thought for tomorrow or yesterday. They lived large in every way and used up their resources. Thorn is a natural defense, but it can also cause harm to the careless and unwary. MEANINGS: Thor's rune; abundance and good times with no thought for the future; chaos; unformed energies; uncontrolled or unharnessed power; possibility of waste of resources or abilities unless harnessed to a purpose or will; unfocused or uncontrolled activity; banishing giants, trolls, orcs, etc., by dissipating the spirit; a crude Thor's hammer or thorn; defense, but also with ability to harm without care taken; base sex; a warning of danger ahead; protection; self-deception; inner truth.

4) Ansuz (Aesir, the mouth): ᚫ

The Aesir were the gods that destroyed the old uncontrolled chaotic world of the giants to make room for the controlled and ordered world of man. MEANINGS: Ash tree connected with Yggdrasil, the world tree; the breath of life, spreading energy throughout the cosmos; right action in accordance with the cosmos; communication and interpersonal relationships with the Divine; getting the message out effectively; information that needs to be shared; information that is kept secret, to the detriment of others; understanding the subtle content of messages and ideas; propaganda; gaining prestige from what you are doing; the staff of Odin; learning; wise counsel; divine aid.

5) Raidho (riding, wagon, and Heimdall): ᚱ

Heimdall created order in society with the Norse class system. Riding was the main means of effective travel. MEANINGS: Movement toward an envisioned goal; right movement; travel with a purpose as opposed to travel for pure recreation; the greatest journey begins with a single step, that first step; lack of or blocked movement; the gathering of resources to travel or accomplish a goal; soul or astral travel; a conveyance—something used for travel; decisive action; communication; your spiritual path.

6) Ken/Kenaz (torch, fire, or need-fire): ᚲ

Fire is the element of warmth and energy, and need-fire was specially kindled for the purpose of dispelling darkness and bringing enlightenment. Knowledge and wisdom were used to create a plan, and then strength was used to accomplish the plan. MEANINGS: Learning to benefit all; the honing and application of skills and abilities; teaching, learning, mentoring, apprenticeship; building things and ideas to advance and make life better for all; the knowledge to defeat a foe; the knowledge of good and evil, of right and harmful action; the thirst and lifelong quest for learning and the passing-on of knowledge; bringing light into dark places; inspiration, mind, and thought; understanding; ideas; inner guidance.

7) Gifu (gift): ᚷ

Gifting as an exchange of energies, you give something and you gain something in return. MEANINGS: Giving and receiving; balanced energies; a sacrifice to the gods in exchange for favors given; "a gift demands a gift," passing along of benefits; you help me and I'll help someone else down the road; diplomacy; negotiation as a true exchange of interests and needs; shared

resources for the common good; obligation; favors given and received; things are done for mutual benefit; initiating and continuing relationships; sharing; success; tolerance; union; happiness.

8) Wunjo (joy): ᚹ

The joy gained in successful creation, the joy of having a wish granted. Having the will to dream and the will to win. MEANINGS: Gaining inner understanding; the ability to truly discern motivation and ambition; overwhelming ambition, sometimes to the detriment of the group; a good time; happy fellowship; the ability to get right with yourself; the end of delusion; the envisioning of desires; the achievement of wishes; family; fellowship; harmony; inner peace.

Hagall's Aett

9) Hagalaz (hail, Hel): ᚺ

The goddess Hel was half alive and half dead. She was neutral in the conflict of Ragnarok, doing things to benefit both sides. Hail is half ice, half water, and considered the worst weapon of the ice giants. MEANINGS: Being between the worlds; neutrality; deterrent; destruction that clears the way for renewal; force that keeps harm away; those who perform the less-desirable tasks that are necessary; traveling the darker roads of the world. Because hail is called the ice seed, and because Balder (among others) will return after Ragnarok, hidden mysteries; connected with prophecy and the Norn Urd—the past; temporary setback; inner crisis; endurance; transformation.

10) Naudiz (need): ᚾ

"Need" as in help and also the need that drives you. Can have the abilities of all the other runes, so can be used in an emergency. MEANINGS: Doing what must be done, or necessary action; having the ability to meet and conquer any situation; having abundant resources to be able to adapt to anything; being prepared for any situation; the freedom that arises from anticipating and being prepared to meet any situation or emergen-

cy; doing something—even if it's wrong, it will turn out all right in the end; the ability to create your own happy ending through your own resources; connected with prophecy and the Norn Skuld—the future; self-restraint; need for patience; simplification.

11) Isa (ice): ᛁ

Another weapon of the frost giants. MEANINGS: A stable or static situation; something that shows potential or might be developed into resources for the future; resources that are permanently locked away, out of reach, or will never be developed; a situation that is not moving at present but that might develop over time into something flowing and useful; a situation that is comfortably at rest and that over time can develop into movement or change, which can be unfortunate or destructive; a blockage or barrier; limitations; potential energy, or energy held in reserve; "now is all there is!" connected with prophecy and the Norn Verdandi—the present, as our concept of "now," is a moment in time; caution, surrender; introspection.

12) Jera (harvest, year): ᛃ

Connected with the Vanir fertility gods Freyr and Freya. MEANINGS: The progression of the seasons; a regulator of action—slows down fast things and speeds up slow things; a positive feedback loop; easy, gentle action; gradual and acceptable change; good things started, spread around, and coming to fruition to create more good; general fertility; the exploration of safely hidden secrets; prophecy as in delving into the hidden mysteries; reward; maturity; right action.

13) Eihwaz (yew tree): ᛇ

A death wood connected with Yggdrasil, the world tree. MEANINGS: An active rune; initiating action in response to something; active protection; movement in response to some situation; necessary killing, as in the execution of a criminal or killing of an animal for food; power activated; the unleashing of potential energy (contrasted with Isa's potential energy); protection in the magickal realm; problem solving; strength under attack; transcendence.

14) *Pertho (secret, birth, dice cup):* ⛤

The dance of creation and destruction; the anvil laid on its side at the end of a day's work. MEANINGS: Building up and creating for the sake of creation; the energy that is the opposite of entropy and that animates the universe; use it to discern group motivations (as opposed to individual motivations); can access racial memory, tribal memory, family memory, or cultural memory; the building of a world, a life; connected to the Norns as a group, also prophecy, and you may also have access to Urd's Well, which—like the Mimir, the well of the Aesir god of wisdom—can be used to access the collective unconscious; fate and rebirth; possible luck, chance and fortune gained; secrets, synchronicity; feminine mysteries.

15) *Elhaz (protection):* ᛉ

A splayed hand, with fingers spread and ready to catch whatever comes your way. Symbol of the Valkyries and also the Rainbow Bridge between Midgard and Asgard. MEANINGS: A warning to keep away; a psychic fence or shield, especially from attacks from unexpected directions; calling for help from others or higher powers or authorities; the veil between the worlds, which must exist if we are able to be distanced from the spiritual, astral, etc., and as a two-way means of traversing the veil; questions of both a bipolar or neutral intent; can be used to counter magick; the need to stay alert; persistence; divine intervention; mysticism.

16) *Sowilo (sun, sun snake, continuing or repeated journey):* ᛋ

A fire rune. MEANINGS: A stabilizing rune, not static but action to stabilize; helps maintain the status quo; stabilizes other runes so they can direct their energies to a specific place or need; intensifies energies; being in the sun is a comfortable pleasant place to be, materially, emotionally, and psychically; a reluctance to change because of the pleasant place where you are—this can lead to comfortable or arrogant indolence; the binding of a spell; the grounding of excess energies, especially if these excess energies are coming up from the ground; final touches making things nice and completed; the end of a long journey; connected with Ragnarok—the ending and beginning of a cycle; victory; vitality; blessing; wholeness.

Tyr's Aett

17) *Tiwaz (Tyr, Tyr's arrow or spear):* ᛏ

Tyr is the god of law but not necessarily justice; he is also the god of war and victory. He can balance the sides to ensure a fair fight, but he also demands total destruction of the enemy. Possibly connected with Irminsul, another depiction of the world tree. MEANINGS: Use of resources to gain victory, advancement, material betterment; the principle of societal correctness; societal mechanisms for controlling or correcting wrong actions; societal conventions and constraints; actions for the betterment of society as a whole; what one needs to do to fit into a society; conformity and conforming; strength and honor; authority; drive; greater good.

18) *Berkano (birch tree):* ᛒ

Associated with Yggdrasil, the world tree, possibly the feminine counterpart to Irminsul. MEANINGS: Associated with women, birthing, children, and healing; the regenerative forces of nature; growth to a desired end; actions that heal, make better, cause to grow, nurture, etc; a happy rune; initiation; the inability to stay the same in the face of a changing and nurturing environment; a safe place to heal and grow; evolution, custom, the habits of a society; justice and making things right, even if it may violate the letter of the law; creativity; new ideas; feminine creative energy.

19) *Ehwaz (horse or pair of horses):* ᛖ

Horses were the main means of land transportation. MEANINGS: The loyalty owed from rider to horse and vice versa; a love rune; relationships that are not of blood or kin; the possibility of friendship, ties by mutual interests or shared outlook; the concept of loyalty outside of kinship, loyalty not of blood but of some-

thing wider; towns and regions of people, groups of families, tribes and groups of tribes; alliances for common interests; motive power; favor of the gods; good omen for a journey; a new start; cooperation; travel; partnership; progress.

20) Mannaz (man): ᛗ

Two men meeting face to face with their hands on each other's shoulders. MEANINGS: Man as the tribe or group, or all of mankind; social intercourse; can help in dealings with others; greasing the social wheels; gain admiration of peers; meeting face-to-face and getting things straight between two people; litigation and negotiations; can be used to arbitrate or mediate a conflict; one-on-one communication; working yourself up to being the equal of any you meet and treating all others as equals with respect and admiration; the ability to discern, nurture, and develop the abilities and strengths of others; the possibility of meeting with people outside immediate family or friends; village meeting village; tribes meeting and dealing; trade issues; deals with the mind and intellect; charitable deeds; transcendence; family; friendship.

21) Laguz (water, flowing): ᛚ

Associated with the Vanir, fertility gods. MEANINGS: Water as a way of travel and source of food; making things smooth; an expediter, a fixer, a go-between; can be used to send or direct energy in whatever direction is needed; shows a developing situation; can give inspiration; can show when inspiration will come and under what circumstances, depending on the other runes around it; following the path of least resistance to attain a goal; go with the flow; let the universe guide your actions; diplomacy; successful and ongoing trade; lasting relationships; treaties; deep mysteries; dreams and visions; abundance worked for; intuition; fluidity; premonitions; unconscious desires.

22) Ing/Ingwaz (a shield): ᛜ,◇

Connected with the Vanir gods of the sea. MEANINGS: Showing familial connections; integrating various parts into a whole; being between the worlds; integrating groups and families, villages, towns, and regions into kingdoms or nations; the establishment of the mechanisms for government over a wide area, not immediately accessible by any one person; the ideas and common interests that allow people to bind together; a magickal shield; sex, fertility, and abundance; achievement; completion; unity; creativity; artistic inspiration.

23) Dagaz (day): ᛞ

Fullest expression of fire and also night. Another bridge rune. MEANINGS: The third eye; spiritual awakening; a realization; a coming of understanding or initiation; national and cultural identity; the day-to-day activities of a people that allow them to live, work, and thrive together; specialization of skills and interests; the Wyrds of Fate; the awakening that the transformation of death can bring; a new beginning; a new day is dawning; a good state of mind can make life satisfying; clarity; relief; progress; destiny.

24) Othala (homeland, noble or inherited wealth): ᛟ

A rune of gathering in. MEANINGS: Assessing your possessions, skills, and abilities; being grateful for what you have and counting your blessings; being in a safe, secure place with all you need, then attracting whatever you want to you; feeling comfortable in a culture; the realization of nationalism, patriotism; the creation of societal wealth, group riches; the establishment of taxes, communication, bureaucracy, and all that is necessary for a society to function well; "united we stand, divided we fall"; the passing along of wealth to descendants or other members of society; the continuity of wealth and ownership; the creation of a stable society that allows for steady accumulation and passing along of wealth; centering, grounding and earthing; responsibilities; universal truths.

THE MAGICK of ASTROLOGY

ASTROLOGY IS A predictive system that uses the twelve constellations along the zodiac and the planets that move within those bounds. It was formulated from roughly 100 BCE to 300 CE, mostly in and around Alexandria, Egypt, which was the center of the scientific world at that time.

The twelve astrological signs were created from various building blocks of meaning, four elements, and three modes of action.

The Elements

Fire △

The element of inspiration—enthusiasm, spirituality, energy, heat, light, actual fire and burning, active, animals, hot and dry.

Air △

The element of mentality—thoughts and movement, communication, actual air and wind, moderately active, humanity, hot and wet.

Water ▽

The element of emotion and feelings—adaptability, psychic abilities, nurturing, actual water that can freeze or flow or turn to steam, passive, plants, cold and wet.

Earth ▽

The element of stability and material manifestation—stubborn, immovable, practical, growing, stable, grounding, passive, actual earth, rocks and crystals, cold and dry. Earth is the immovable object.

There is a fifth element—Spirit—which is pure heat, the medium through which all the energies of astrology manifest in the world. It infuses and penetrates everything. Spirit is the irresistible force. It is extremely important, but because it is everywhere, it is largely ignored except as how the energies of the signs and planets work upon us all.

The Three Modes of Action

Cardinal
The mode of leadership—decisive, active, initiating, beginning, progressive, future oriented, goal oriented, may act before thought, energetic, forward thinking.

Fixed
The mode of practicality—stability, fixity, reactive, sustaining, grounded, conservative, past oriented, ending, reward oriented, thinks but may not act, methodical and backward thinking.

Mutable
The mode of adaptability—interactive, accommodating, following, communicating, facilitating, process oriented, moderate, present oriented, think and act in equal proportions, flexible and creative thinking.

The Signs

Mix the four elements with the three modes and you get twelve possibilities, with each combination unique.

Aries the Ram (cardinal fire—I am—aspiration—ruled by the planet Mars): ♈
Aries moves forward full speed ahead; anyone else can catch up. Aries is direct, somewhat guileless and naive; there is a childlike quality of enthusiasm and optimism, with endless curiosity and a fearless way of going forward where others might pause and consider. Aries can get angry and make a great noise but also calms down just as quickly and wonders why others are still worked up. The sign of beginnings, fearless action, new endeavors, spontaneity, momentum, initiative, confidence, strong will, courage, military, and risk.

Taurus the Bull (fixed earth—I have—integration—ruled by the planet Venus): ♉
Taurus is quiet, conservative, and artistic in a material way. They prize their creature comforts, comfort foods, and simple, satisfying pleasures. They are usually calm and placid but are capable of being the bull in the china shop when finally angered to action. They are stubborn and steady. They have endless patience and can accumulate great wealth; by building things slowly, they can gain a great deal. Taurus is the sign of rootedness, abundance, fertility, physical comforts and material possessions, patience, endurance, determination to see things through, the ability to stay focused, loyalty, being a connoisseur.

Gemini the Twins (mutable air—I think—vivification—ruled by the planet Mercury): ♊
Gemini is versatile, active, gregarious, talkative, and endlessly curious. They love being around people and may have many friends. Gemini accumulates information and may enjoy telling stories, reporting or teaching what they have seen and heard. They may move from place to place and can be restless if they are forced to stay still. The sign of travel, communication, ideas, swift thought, clever words, writing, thievery, trade, doubt, and questioning.

Cancer the Crab (cardinal water—I feel—expansion—ruled by the Moon): ♋
Cancer is emotional and can be moody but also sensitive and empathic. They are quietly but patiently ambitious. They prize security and will endure a great deal in order to keep that security. They can also accumulate wealth, but as a hedge against adversity and want. The sign of security, mother and mothering, nurturing and caring, psychic abilities, mediumship, family, home, instinct, protection of others, devotion, history, gentle mocking humor, romance, and sentimentality.

Leo the Lion (fixed fire—I will—assurance—ruled by the sun): ♌
Leo loves being the center of attention and living large. Leo loves the grand gesture and is open and generous. There is a fun-loving thread that runs through most everything Leo does. Leo plans and organizes on a large scale. Their self-confidence can turn to braggadocio if they feel unappreciated. The sign of optimism, ego, royal actions, fun and games, entertainment, confidence, self-expression, joy, luxury, generosity, slapstick humor, goofiness, living large, and theatre.

Virgo the Virgin (mutable earth—I analyze—assimilation—ruled by the planet Mercury): ♍

Virgo is practical, discerning, and exacting. They may seem prissy and reserved, but their sensuality is there—just carefully hoarded for times when appropriate, and then they let go. This sign prefers getting their chores done before having fun, otherwise they'd worry about what needs doing. The scientific method is a Virgo pursuit. The sign of discernment, careful action, skill and detail, practical pursuits, logical thought, patient creativity, perfect servant or aide, craft schools, health and wellness, and economics.

Libra the Scales or Balance (cardinal air—I balance—equilibrium—ruled by the planet Venus): ♎

Libra loves peace and tranquility and is happiest when in a partnership. They can have trouble making up their minds, wanting to hear all the options and opinions of others before making a decision. Libra loves art and music and prefers to live in a beautiful environment. Their ability to weigh and balance makes for a good lawyer. Libra is the sign of peace, balance, fairness and equity, partnership, marriage, those that oppose you openly, war and conflict, diplomacy, compromise, tactics, and luxury.

Scorpio the Scorpion (fixed water—I desire—creativity—ruled by the planets Mars and Pluto): ♏

Sex, death, and rebirth are matters this sign undertakes to know. Secretive and mysterious, Scorpio's hypnotic gaze can mesmerize. Scorpio wants to know all your secrets but will rarely reveal any of their own. Scorpio rules the depths and heights of passion and emotion. They are persistent, which can border on obsessive. Their intensity can make for great achievements. The sign of intensity, unlocking mysteries, obsession, deep feelings, psychic abilities, detecting and discovering things, sexuality and abstinence, espionage, depth and extremes, strategy.

Sagittarius the Centaur (mutable fire—I see—administration—ruled by the planet Jupiter): ♐

Sag is happy-go-lucky, a traveler and an adventurer. They want to learn and roam unfettered by ties of responsibility or obligation. They can be profligate or devout and pious—sometimes both at different stages of life. They revere the law and learning. They may sow their wild oats but eventually settle down to a life of devotion and morality. This is the Indiana Jones sign—the sign of adventure, high ideals, travel, learning, foreign cultures, law and justice, judges and priests, colleges and universities.

Capricorn the Goat or Sea-Goat (cardinal earth—I use—discrimination—ruled by the planet Saturn): ♑

Capricorn is determined, relentless, patient, and cautious but always making their way upwards. They are ambitious and sometimes a snob or social climber. They prefer being the power behind the throne. Capricorn prefers real power to the trappings and outward appearances thereof. They accumulate by being frugal and saving, sometimes to the point of miserliness. The sign of practicality, business, achievement, sober reflection, miserliness, dry wit, sharp trader, practical pessimist, lasting values, trustee, sober, prudence, and seriousness.

Aquarius the Water Bearer (fixed air—I know—loyalty—ruled by the planets Saturn and Uranus): ♒

These are the most unconventional people of the zodiac. They resist being pigeon-holed and like to do things their way, no matter if it's socially acceptable or not. They are exciting, sometimes radical, and love mankind and humanity but can find it hard to relate to people one-on-one. There is a detached air that may make them seem cold and unfeeling, but they prefer rational logical thinking to emotional persuasion. This is the Mr. Spock sign. The sign of innovation, wild ideas that may actually work, thinking outside the box, optimism, hippy, freedom, equality for all, utopia, advertising, public relations, and anarchy.

Pisces the Fishes (mutable water—I believe—appreciation—ruled by the planets Jupiter and Neptune): ♓

Sensitive, psychic, and emotional, Pisces can mimic the other signs through their deep understanding of people and their motivations. They can seem timid and shy but have a deep empathy and love of others that can manifest as sacrificing themselves for the sake of the other's good. Sometimes they can live in their own little world, safe from the harsh realities of life. But they can also step up when needed and tackle big issues for the sake of a friend or loved one. The sign of art and creativity, charity, fantasy, selfless lover, spiritual advisor, surrender, deep connection with deity or the universe, martyr, pharmaceuticals, photography, and movies.

The Planets

The planets are forces that operate through the filter of the signs. Each planet has a sign (or signs) that they are at home in and are more or less comfortable in. The planets have their own distinct natures, but those natures can be expressed for good or ill depending on what signs they are placed in, how effectively they operate in the sign they are in, and how they interact with other planets.

Sun ☉

The Greater Light, the King of the Day, the center of the solar system, its fiery rays can warm or burn depending on the season. Ruler of Leo, exalted in Aries. Hot and dry, the sun rules the masculine principle and men in general, though specifically men in their strong middle age, after thirty, when they are mature and most effective. He rules ego, energy, honor and standing, those who rule, pride, awards, will and willpower. He rules rulers, goldsmiths, noble professions, nobility, father, yang, male energy, authority, organizers, consciousness, motivation, optimism, personality, hero's journey, role models, honor.

Moon ☽

The Lesser Light, the Queen of the Night, she reflects the light of the sun, cooling and moderating the sun's fiery energy. Ruler of Cancer, exalted in Taurus. Cool and watery, the moon rules the feminine principle and females and women in general, from maidens to mothers to crones. She also rules young children from birth to school age. She rules emotions, memory, liquids, fishing, sailors, any who make their living by waters or the sea, mediums and psychic activity, yin, feminine energy, inner nature, realm of feelings, mother, family, imagination, fantasy, the population at large, home, unconscious, longing for closeness and security.

Mercury ☿

The messenger of the zodiac, Mercury moves between the other planets, communicating and passing along information. Ruler of Gemini and Virgo, exalted in Virgo (Mercury really loves being in Virgo). Mercury's nature is mutable, taking on the characteristics of the sign it is in and the planets it aspects. He rules children from school age to puberty. Mercury rules communication, thought and mentality, travel and movement, conveyances, and speech. He rules people who make their living by their words, short journeys (cabs and so forth), writing, thievery, scouting and reconnaissance, ideas, siblings, reading and writing, students, and adaptability.

Venus ♀

The Lesser Benefic, a social planet. Ruler of Taurus and Libra, exalted in Pisces. Warm and moist, Venus's nature has changed through the ages depending on the nature of women in society. With the moon, she rules the feminine principle, though more that of the maiden—from puberty to becoming a desirable woman and fertile partner. Venus is the planet of love, romance, art, and beauty. Sensuous and enticing, Venus can be passive, lazy, and indolent because it's easier to have fun than work hard. She gives nice things if

well aspected. She rules manners, deportment, and politeness, the things that make a social group work well together. She rules song and music, that which is pleasant and uplifting. She rules agriculture, horticulture, harmony, aesthetics, balance, sensory pleasures, eroticism, and sexual attraction.

Mars ♂

The Lesser Malefic, a social planet. Ruler of Aries and Scorpio, exalted in Capricorn. Hot and dry, Mars rules the masculine principle with the sun, though more of young men from puberty to about thirty, in their physical prime and ready to take on the world. He has always been about energy, anger, conflict, ego, courage, and action. Mars prefers to be active and aggressive. Loud and persistent, Mars will not be quiet when he feels the need to be heard. Mars rules war, conflict, action, and explosions. He rules soldiers, the military, and police. He rules wounds, blood, conquerors, war, passion, the sex act itself, sexual satisfaction, passion, violence, entrepreneurs, adventurers, tyrants, and goal-oriented people.

Jupiter ♃

The Greater Benefic, a societal planet. Ruler of Sagittarius and Pisces, exalted in Cancer. Hot and moist, Jupiter is the largest planet in the solar system and is masculine, ruling the male past fifty or so in his later grand statesman/philosopher time of life. He is all about expansion, abundance, wealth, mercy, and honor. He gives good things and loves a good time. He is the judge who tempers justice with mercy. He rules religion, the clergy, legislatures and assemblies, publishing, lawyers and judges, professors, philosophers, scholars, athletes, fortune and fulfillment, world travelers, truth, justice, principles and values, trust, goodness, and goodwill.

Saturn ♄

The Greater Malefic, a societal planet. Ruler of Capricorn and Aquarius, exalted in Libra. Cold and dry, Saturn was the farthest planet visible before telescopes were invented. He is masculine, though he rules men and women from retirement age onward and crones. Saturn is about limitations, boundaries, difficult things, and that which can be attained through hard work and patient persistence. Saturn's rewards come after much hard work, setbacks, and difficult lessons, but they are more enduring and appreciated than the easy gifts of Venus or Jupiter. Saturn rules by the letter of the law—no deviations. He rules boundaries, limitations, debilities, difficulties, and that which limits and blocks. He rules working people, mines and mining, laborers, the working class, structure, steadfastness, stamina, security, time, endings, conscience, obligation, wisdom, and self-control.

The Modern Planets

Uranus, Neptune, and Pluto are called the modern planets. The influences of the modern planets are more collective than personal; some say they rule the collective unconscious, but people with one or more of these planets highlighted in their chart are more in tune with the energies of their times and generation. Sign placement of the modern planets can define generations, and their hard aspects define interesting times. If you respond to their energies, a modern planet transit can bring upheaval to your life and also bring new opportunities and experiences.

Uranus ♅

A universal planet. Co-ruler of Aquarius and exalted in Scorpio. Uranus was discovered at the time of the scientific revolution, the Age of Enlightenment, the rise of democracy, and the understanding of electricity. Uranus's nature is erratic, electric, eccentric, and unpredictable. He rules anarchists, revolutionaries, radio and television, scientific breakthroughs, freedom, equality, brotherhood, independence, sudden change and upheaval, genius, human rights, liberation, inventions, technicians, futurists, eccentrics, and recluses.

Neptune ♆

A universal planet. Co-ruler of Pisces and exalted in Cancer. Neptune was discovered during the Romantic Age—the time of the humanistic backlash to strict scientific thought and analysis. Neptune represents the principle of dissolving boundaries and is the planet of illusion, mysticism, psychic awareness, and the ability to pierce the veils between the worlds. He can bring enlightenment, union with the Divine, or addiction. Medicine was discovering the use of refined drugs and compounds to alleviate suffering and pain and cure disease. Anesthesia is definitely a Neptunian thing. Neptune has a fuzzy and insubstantial nature. He operates more in the realm of emotions and fluids rather than solid, tangible things. He rules the unconscious and its effects on the psyche, mediums and psychic activity in general, drugs, addiction, hypnosis, spiritual matters, poisons, toxic effects, pollution, idealism, altruism, redemption, melancholy, self-deception, co-dependence, chemistry, swindlers, con men, mystics, idealism, communism, and utopia.

Pluto ♇ ♀

A universal planet. Co-ruler of Scorpio and exalted in Aquarius (or maybe Aries—some are still arguing about it). Pluto was demoted from full planetary status in 2005 by scientists who do not believe astrology is a valid worldview. Pluto was discovered at the time of the rise of the modern dictators and ushered in the Atomic Age. Pluto rules mass movements, the mafia and other large criminal organizations, oligarchs, international banking, the underworld, physics, radioactivity, shamanism, deep transformation, sewers and waste treatment, the abyss, obsession, dictatorship, plumbing the depths to cleanse and attain the heights, societal upheaval, mass marketing, propaganda, psychotherapy, sadism, torture, fanaticism, radical transformation, deep research, forbidden teachings, and demagogues.

Earth ⊕

The planet we reside upon. Earth is not shown explicitly but is implied at the center of every astrological chart. The planet Earth can also be used as another symbol for the element of earth.

SPELLWORKING LOG

HERE WE'VE PROVIDED a spellworking log for you to keep track of your results and success—a magickal diary, if you will. This is completely optional! Do this only if it seems helpful. Remember that magick should be fun as well as serious.

DATE	SPELL	DEITIES	IMMEDIATE IMPRESSIONS	RESULTS (WEEK/MONTH/YEAR)

Date	Spell	Deities	Immediate Impressions	Results (week/month/year)

ABOUT THE BOOK

HELGA WAS GOING through a series of life issues. She is an artist and expresses herself artistically. She created a series of drawings loosely based on the first thirteen cards of the Major Arcana of the tarot. These images addressed issues she needed to work through in her life. Each image was created for a magickal purpose, and as she worked through each one, her life improved in that area.

When finished, she collected all the images and created this magickal system whereby you take her images and color your own energies and intent into them to create a complete spell. She asked Estelle to help her with the text part of the book, and you have in your hands the finished collaboration. Later the project was expanded using all twenty-two cards of the Major Arcana and adding the four aces of the four suits of the tarot deck.

Helga and Estelle have been friends and magickal collaborators for many years. They started as teacher and student, and over the years their friendship and magickal accomplishments have grown. This is their first professionally published collaboration.

Helga Hedgewalker

Helga Hedgewalker is a visionary artist, Gardnerian High Priestess, and Witch with decades of professional experience in print design, illustration, book design, package design, web graphics, and advertising. She is a founding member of the Minneapolis Collective of Pagan Artists (visit them at facebook.com/MPLSCPA) and co-owner of the Spirit Parlour, a shop and blog of magic, mysticism, and spirituality that can be found at SpiritParlour.com.

In her spare time Helga works in large-scale painting on canvas, digital collage, costuming, and designing coloring books. Her recent works can be seen at HelgaHedgewalker.com. She also loves creating ritual tools, making seasonal crafts, and swimming. Someday she plans to become a mermaid and swim far away…

Her creative works are offerings of beauty to the gods.

> *The more beauty there is to see,*
> *the more your soul is fed.*
> *The more your soul is fed,*
> *the more sacred and balanced*
> *your life will become.*
> *It is one of the paths to the center.*

Estelle Daniels

Estelle is author of *Astrologickal Magick* (Weiser, 1995), a guide to timing your life using astrology, and co-author of *Pocket Guide to Wicca* (Crossing Press, 1998) and *Essential Wicca* (Crossing Press, 2001), books on the religion and practice of Wicca, written with her late spouse, Paul Tuitean. She also wrote *Tarot Lore and Other B.S.* (Jester Studio Press, 2014), *Breaking the Rules Tarot: The Book of Interpretations* (Jester Studio Press, 2016), and *Practical Tylering: A Field Magick Manual* (Jester Studio Press, 2017). She co-designed *Breaking the Rules Tarot Deck* with Peggy McDowell (Jester Studio Press, 2016).

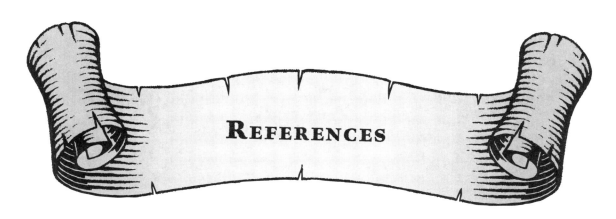

REFERENCES

Banzhaf, Hajo, and Anna Haebler. *Key Words for Astrology.* York Beach, ME: Samuel Weiser, 1996.

Eversden, Lona. *Rune Oracle.* Oceana.

Tauring, Kari. *The Runes: A Human Adventure.* 2007.

Tuitean, Paul, and Estelle Daniels. *The Rune Book.* 1997, unpublished.

BRIGHT BLESSINGS!

May all your magickal dreams take wing.

much love,
Helga & Estelle